The Magician's Nephew

A guide to C. S. Lewis' Novel
By
Shan Gillard

Copyright © 2011 Novel Insights Plus

All rights reserved.

ISBN: 10: 1477649654

ISBN-13: 13:978-1477649657

Dedication:
This book is dedicated to all who love the teaching of the story of Aslan and the truth of Who He is.

TABLE OF CONTENTS

Author Biography... 1

Chapter 1..3

Chapters 2-3..11

Chapter 4...17

Chapters 5-6..25

Chapters 7-8..32

Chapter 9...41

Chapters 10-11..49

Chapters 12-13..57

Chapters 14-15..67

Vocabulary Tests...74

Test Questions..91

Vocabulary Crossword Puzzle..99

Selected Bibliography...113

AUTHOR BIOGRAPHY

Clive Staples Lewis (known to his friends as "Jack") was born on November 29, 1898, in Belfast, Northern Ireland to Albert J. and Florence Lewis. His brother Warren (Warnie) was three years older than he. In 1905 the family moved to their new home, "Little Lea," on the outskirts of Belfast.

Flora Lewis died of cancer in 1908, and Jack entered Wynyard School in England, where his brother Warnie had been attending since 1905. Due to respiratory problems, he was enrolled in Campbell College, Belfast in 1910, and eventually sent to Cherbourg School, Malvern, England in 1911. Malvern was famous as a health resort, and Warnie was enrolled at Malvern College. While at boarding school, Jack was introduced to the occult by one of his teachers, and eventually became an atheist.

In 1914 Lewis met Arthur Greeves, who, next to his brother, became his closest friend. He also began to study under W.T. Kirkpatrick ("The Great Knock"), and in 1916 won a scholarship to Oxford College. He was a student at Oxford from April 26 until September of 1916.

Lewis enlisted in the British army and was billeted in Keble College, Oxford, for officer's training. His roommate was Edward Courtnay Francis "Paddy" Moore. Lewis was wounded during the Battle of Arras on April 15, 1918, was returned to duty in October, and discharged in December 1918. Paddy Moore was killed in battle. "Death in Battle," published in the February, 1919 issue of *Reveille*, was Lewis' first published work. From January 1919 until June 1924 he resumed his studies at Oxford.

In 1920, Paddy Moore's mother and sister moved to Oxford, and Lewis lived with them from June 1921 on. In 1930 they purchased "The Kilns." The title to the property belonged to Mrs. Moore, with both Jack and Warren Lewis having rights of life tenancy.

From October 1924 until May 1925, Lewis served as philosophy tutor at University College. In May he was elected a Fellow of Magdalen College, Oxford, where he served as a tutor in English language and Literature until 1954.

In 1931 Lewis became a Christian after having had a long talk with two of his friends, J.R.R. Tolkien and Hugo Dyson. The talk took place in the evening, and is recorded in *They Stand Together*. Lewis recorded the following day's events in *Surprised by Joy*: "When we (Warnie and Jack) set out (by motorcycle to the Whipsnade Zoo) I did not believe that Jesus Christ was the Son of God, and when we reached the zoo I did."

In 1933, Lewis began having regular meetings with a group of friends who were writers, calling themselves the Inklings. Included in this group were J.R.R. Tolkien, Lewis' brother Warren, Hugo Dyson, Charles Williams, Dr. Robert Havard, Owen Barfield, Weville Coghill and others.

Lewis became a prolific writer and a leading apologist (one who defends the Christian faith). He published *The Screwtape Letters* in 1941, *The Abolition of Man* in 1943, *Mere Christianity* and *The Great Divorce* in 1945. *Out of the Silent Planet*, the first novel in his Space Trilogy, was published in 1938; *Perelandra*, the second novel of the Trilogy, in 1943, and *That Hideous Strength* in 1945.

Of course, *The Chronicles of Narnia*, a series of seven books which continue to enjoy tremendous popularity, was published between 1950 and 1956. The concept for *The Chronicles of Narnia* was born when Lewis opened his home to some of the English children who were sent to live in the countryside in order to escape the bombing of the British cities. Some of the children became fascinated with a wardrobe in his home, believing it led to another world. Having read about such a magic wardrobe when he was a child in *The Aunt and Anabel* by Edith Nesbit, he was captivated by the idea.

In 1952 Lewis met Joy Davidman Gresham, who was fifteen years his junior, for the first time. She had converted to Christianity from Judaism in 1948 in part as a result of reading his books. They were married in a secret civil ceremony in 1956 when the British Home Office denied continuance of her residency permit. In 1957, a bedside ceremony was performed in accordance with the Church of England, because they believed her death from bone cancer was imminent. However, her cancer went into remission, and she lived until 1960.

Till We Have Faces was published in 1956. It was Lewis' last novel, and he considered it to be his best, although the critics did not agree with him. The book used the mythological story of Psyche and Cupid as a vehicle to convey the everlasting and precious truths of the gospel.

C.S. Lewis left the Shadowlands of this world at 5:30 P.M. on November 22, 1963, the same day that President John F. Kennedy was assassinated in Dallas, TX. Although American history continues to be ambivalent concerning President Kennedy's impact, it can be said without the least hesitation that the influence of C.S. Lewis will turn minds and hearts to Christ well into the twenty-first century.

CHAPTER 1

Chapter one provides the setting for the story as well as the importance of imparting this information – it explains how Narnia began. By using the "days Mr. Sherlock Holmes was still living in Baker Street" as a time marker, the actual time placement for this story would be late nineteenth/early twentieth century. At this point in time, there lived in London a young girl named Polly Plumber and a boy named Digory. Polly is surprised one day to discover Digory living next door to her, as there have been no children living there before. However, he has come to live with his Uncle Andrew and Aunt Letty Ketterly, a bachelor and old maid who live next door to Polly. Polly discovers Digory crying in his back yard, and asks him why he is crying. He denies having been crying at first, then admits it, saying anyone who has lived in the country with a pony and a river at the bottom of their garden would cry if they had to come to live in a hole like London while their father was away in India. He goes on to explain his mother is ill and is going to die. Trying to distract him, Polly asks if his uncle is really mad. He replies that he is either mad or has some mystery going on in his top floor study where no one is allowed to enter, not even his Aunt Letty. Furthermore, every time his uncle attempts to speak to him at meals, Aunt Letty shuts him up. Digory mentions he is sure he heard a yell as he passed the attic stairs the night before, and Polly suggests perhaps Uncle Andrew keeps a mad wife shut up in the room. Digory counters with the idea that it might be a pirate like in *Treasure Island*. Polly exclaims his house is exciting, but Digory tells her it is scary to sleep there; he finds Uncle Andrew's eyes frightening. Because the summer becomes very wet and cold, the children begin to explore inside their houses, and discover a passageway that connects the two houses through their attics. They talk of the prospect of exploring one of the houses that has been empty for as long as anyone can remember. Neither of them uses the word "haunted," but that is the reputation of the house. Digory thinks someone is living in the house, citing noises that have been heard. Polly reports her father attributes the noises to the drains. They make careful calculations as to how far they should go to take them past Digory's house and into the unoccupied house. However, they are also in a hurry, because they want the adventure to begin. As they reach their destination, they find a small door with no handle, and open it. To their astonishment, instead of finding a deserted room, they discover an attic that is furnished as a sitting room. On a table in the middle of the room is a tray with a number of brightly colored pairs of rings on it. They notice the sound of a ticking clock, as well as a humming sound. Polly is drawn to the rings, but Digory tells her they need to leave before they are found. Before they can withdraw, Digory's Uncle Andrew appears and they realize they are not only in Digory's house, but in Uncle Andrew's forbidden study. Uncle Andrew immediately locks the door, declaring his sister will not be able to interfere with him now. Digory and Polly are filled with fear, and Digory tries to back out the door through which they entered, but Uncle Andrew is too quick, shutting and locking that door as well. Polly pleads with him to let them go, promising they will return after dinner if he will allow them to leave. He tells them he was hoping for some children for an experiment he was conducting. He has used a guinea pig, but now needs some children. Digory reminds him it is dinner time, and they will be missed. He must let them go. Andrew will not be coerced. He feigns giving in to them, telling them he will give them a present before they go, and offers Polly one of the yellow rings. She asks about the green ones, but he tells her he cannot give her one of the green ones; only one of the yellow ones. Polly observes the humming sound seems louder closer to the rings, almost as if they are making the sound. As she reaches for the ring, Digory admonishes her not to be a fool and touch them. However, it is too late. As Polly touches the ring, she disappears, leaving only Digory and Uncle Andrew in the room.

SUGGESTED ACTIVITIES CHAPTER 1

1. Ask students to illustrate in the manner of their choosing the main characters of the story who have been introduced thus far: Polly, Digory and Uncle Andrew.

2. Have students read one of the *Sherlock Holmes* stories and come to a conclusion as to the time period in which the story is set. Ask them why they think C.S. Lewis used Sherlock Holmes as a time marker, rather than simply giving the actual date. (Hint: Lewis was writing for British schoolchildren, all of whom would have been familiar with Sherlock Holmes and the time period in which his stories were set. Many of today's American students, on the other hand, are not even familiar with Holmes. Explain that this was more creative and allowed the reader to use his deductive abilities.)

3. Ask students to write a short story about children exploring an area that is familiar to them in the beginning, which leads to something surprising at the end. This could be something that has happened to them in real life, or something they create from their imagination.

VOCABULARY CHAPTER 1

Bastables:		a fictional family written about by Edith Nesbit in *The Story of the Treasure Seekers* and *The Wouldbegoods*
Eton:		the largest and most famous of England's public schools
vain:	(adj)	futile; unsuccessful
beastly:	(adj)	abominable; disagreeable
indignantly:	(adv)	expressing strong displeasure at something considered unjust, offensive, insulting
mad:	(adj)	disordered in mind; insane
fishy:	(adj)	questionable
coiner:	(v)	inventer
cistern:	(n)	an often underground tank for storing water
smugglers:	(n)	one who import or export secretly, illegally, or without paying the duties required by law
draughty:	(adj)	characterized by or admitting currents of air, usually uncomfortable
bunk:	(v)	to run off or away; flee
tousled:	(adj)	disheveled; mussed
cunning:	(adj)	marked by wiliness and trickery
duffer:	(n)	an incompetent or clumsy person

The Magician's Nephew

QUESTIONS CHAPTER 1

1. The setting of a novel tells the time and place in which it occurs. What is the setting of *The Magician's Nephew*?

2. Why does the author feel it is important to tell this story?

3. In comparing the time in which the story is set to the time in which he is writing, how does the author contrast the two?

4. Describe Polly and Digory.

5. Why is Polly surprised the first time she meets Digory?

6. Where has Digory lived before? Why is he living where he is now? How does he feel about his present situation?

7. What seems to be the general reputation of Digory's Uncle Andrew?

8. What does Digory say about him?

9. What happens that causes the children to explore inside the house? What do they discover?

10. Why do they want to explore the house on the other side of Polly's?

11. Although neither of them says it, what explanation do they think might explain why the house has been empty so long? How does Polly's father explain the strange noises that come from the house?

12. As they reach the place they calculate will take them to the empty house, what do they find?

13. What surprises them on the other side?

14. Before they can escape, who greets them? What does he do that they find disturbing?

15. Why does he say he has been wanting two children?

16. What do they try to convince him to do?

17. In what way does he seem to change?

18. What does he offer to Polly?

19. Read Gen. 3:1-6. How does Uncle Andrew's offer of the rings to Polly compare to the temptation of Eve by the serpent?

20. What does Polly find she feels about the rings? What does that say about temptation?

21. Which rings does he tell her she may not choose from?

22. What does Polly notice about the rings as she draws nearer?

23. Although Polly is no longer frightened by Uncle Andrew, what does Digory notice that causes him alarm?

24. Why does Polly not heed Digory's warning?

25. What does Polly have to do with the ring in order for it to work its magic?

The Magician's Nephew

ANSWERS TO QUESTIONS CHAPTER 1

1. It takes place in London, England during the late 1800s and early 1900s.

2. This story explains how Narnia first began.

3. He says that the schools were nastier, but the meals were nicer, and the sweets were good and cheap.

4. Polly is a young girl of school age who has been living in London, apparently for her entire life. She is very curious, has an active imagination, and a longing for adventure. Digory is a boy about the same age as Polly who has lived in the country but has come to live in the city with his aunt and uncle. He also is well read, curious and desirous of adventure. He is grieving because his father is in India and is mother is ill with a terminal illness. He welcomes the imaginative adventures with Polly, which provide a distraction from the loss he is feeling.

5. There has never been a child living in that house; only the Ketterleys, who are a bachelor and his old maid sister.

6. He lived in the country before, but has come to stay with his aunt and uncle because his father is in India and his mother is dying. He is grieving the loss of his life in the country, his separation from his father, and his mother's illness and imminent death.

7. It is believed he is insane.

8. Either he is insane or there is some other mystery going on with him, since he has a room in the attic which he will not allow anyone else to enter. Digory says he is sure he has heard a yell coming from the room, and Polly suggests perhaps Uncle Andrew keeps an insane wife locked in the room, or maybe he is a pirate or an inventor.

9. The weather is more cold and rainy than usual for the summer, and they are forced to play inside. Polly has been playing in the attic for some time, and they discover the attics of all the houses are connected.

10. The house has been empty ever since Polly's family has lived there.

11. They think the house might be haunted. He attributes the noises to drain pipes.

12. They find a small door with no handle on their side – it was made for getting into the crawl space above the attic, not getting out of it.

13. Instead of opening into an empty house, the door opens into a furnished room.

14. Uncle Andrew greets them, then locks the door in order to prevent them from escaping. He also locks the small door through which they have entered, blocking any hope of escape.

15. He has been in the middle of an experiment which he has tried on a guinea pig, and he needs some children to further test the experiment.

16. They try to convince him to let them go to eat dinner, then come back to him after dinner.

17. He suddenly seems more friendly and softer toward them, acting as if he will actually let them go.

18. He offers her one of the rings on the table.

19. Just as Eve finds the fruit pleasant to the eye and something to be desired, Polly is drawn to the rings, finding them beautiful and attractive.

20. Polly finds the rings very attractive. Those things that are sinful never appear repulsive. They always draw us to them by their attractiveness.

21. He tells her she may only choose one of the yellow ones, not one of the green ones.

22. She notices a humming sound that seems to get louder as she gets nearer to the rings.

23. He notices an eager, almost greedy look in his eyes.

24. The attraction of the rings is too great.

25. She only has to touch it – she does not have to put it on.

CHAPTERS 2-3

Andrew explains that, once he had devised the yellow and green rings, he felt quite sure that a yellow ring would transport any creature that touched it to another world. However, the difficulty was in having them tell him what the other world was like. Digory asks why Andrew doesn't just send himself to the other world so he can find out for himself what it is like. Andrew is shocked and offended at Digory's suggestion, dismissing it as preposterous that one in his position in life would risk his health to do such a thing. Digory replies he is a coward to have sent a girl like Polly to face dangers that he himself is afraid to face. Andrew silences him, exclaiming that he is the scholar and scientist, and they are his subjects. The next thing Digory will be saying is that Andrew should have asked permission of the guinea pig before he sent him. Digory asks again if Andrew is going to bring Polly back, to which he replies that a green ring is necessary to draw one back for the return journey. Digory observes that Polly was sent without a green ring, which is the same as if Andrew murdered her. Andrew suggests that if someone goes to her bringing her a green ring, she will be able to return. Digory recognizes his uncle has backed him into a corner, and he has no recourse but to accept his proposal. He tells Andrew that he had never believed in magic before, but now he has no choice. This must mean that the old fairy tales have some basis in truth, also. In these, the wicked are always punished, and Digory sees Andrew as the most wicked man he has ever encountered. This is the first thing Digory has said that really gets through to Andrew. He has a momentary look of horror on his face, but quickly recovers.

Donning gloves, Andrew places two green rings into Digory's right pocket. He explains that one must touch the rings with their skin in order for the magic to work. Digory reaches for the yellow ring, then hesitates, asking what Andrew will say if Digory's mother asks where he is. Taunting him, Andrew throws open the door and tells him to leave the poor Plummer girl over there to be eaten by wild animals or drowned or starved, and he can drop in on Mrs. Plummer and explain why her daughter can't return home. Feeling there is no other decent thing to do, Digory buttons up his coat, takes a deep breath, and picks up the ring.

Immediately the study and Uncle Andrew vanishes, and Digory finds himself surfacing from a pool. He crawls up onto a grassy bank, finding himself neither dripping wet nor panting for breath. He is standing at the edge of the small pool in a wood so dense he cannot see the sky through the trees. There is complete silence. There seem to be no animals and no wind, but Digory notices there are dozens of small pools. When asked afterward to describe the place, Digory describes it as a rich place. He immediately forgets where he has come from and why he is here. If anyone were to ask, he would tell them he had always been in this place. After some time, he notices a girl lying on her back a short distance away, and she tells him that she thinks she has seen him before. Digory replies he thinks he has seen her before, too, and asks how long she has been here. She informs him she has always been here, to which he says he has, too. She contradicts him, telling him she saw him come out of the little pool. Digory seems puzzled, and responds that, yes, he thinks he did.

They try to remember their connection, and believe they are mixed up in some sort of dream world when a guinea pig suddenly appears. Taped to the guinea pig is a yellow ring, and at the same moment, Polly shouts, "Mr. Ketterley!" and Digory shouts, "Uncle Andrew!" This allows them to recover their memories, and Polly asks if they should take the guinea pig and return home now. Digory is more reluctant, wanting to stay and enjoy the place where they are. Polly, however, points out that the place is too dream-like. If they lie down and go to sleep, they might sleep forever. Polly insists they must get back, even though it is very pleasant where they are. She first wants to bring the guinea pig, then decides they should leave him where he is, since he seems perfectly happy and is safe from the wicked clutches of Uncle Andrew. Digory wonders how they will get back, and Polly points him to the pool, despairing that she does not have a bathing suit. Digory tells her they do not need one — the pool does not get one wet. Neither is a very good swimmer, and both are reluctant to jump in, but they decide to take the leap. They jump into the water, only to find the water is only ankle deep. When Polly asks what could have gone wrong, Digory remembers the green rings in his pocket. He explains they must remove the yellow rings and put on the green ones. Returning to the pool wearing the green rings, they are about to jump when Digory has another idea. He suggests that, instead of just jumping into the pool from which they came, they explore some of the other pools. He wonders if there is another world at the bottom of every one of the pools. Excitedly, he explains his theory to Polly — the wood in which they have landed is not a world at all, but an in-between place like the tunnel between their houses at home. Ready to begin exploring, Digory asks which pool Polly wants to explore, but she refuses to try any without knowing first they can return to their own world. Digory doesn't want to go back and be caught by Uncle Andrew, but they decide to go part of the way down in order to assure themselves they can make the return journey. They argue over who will yell "change" when they feel they are getting too close to Uncle Andrew's laboratory, but finally take the plunge. As they pass through the pool, they begin to see landmarks of London, and know they are approaching Digory's home. Although everything is vague and shadowy, they can even see Uncle Andrew, and Polly shouts, "Change." They change back to their yellow rings, bringing them back to the wood between the worlds. Before they decide which pool to explore, Polly asks if they are going to mark this pool so they will be able to find it again. Digory takes his pocket knife and digs up the turf near the pool, leaving a gash they can see. They begin to quarrel over which pool they want to explore, finally choosing one and putting on their yellow rings for the outward journey. However, they have the same experience with this pool they had with the other — they jump in only to find it ankle deep. Uncle Andrew has misunderstood the nature of the material from which the rings are made. The yellow rings draw one to the wood, and the green ones draw one away. They decide to try the green rings, and once more jump into the pool.

The Magician's Nephew

SUGGESTED ACTIVITES CHAPTERS 2-3

1. Have students draw or make a model of their impression of the Wood Between the Worlds.

2. Uncle Andrew is obviously a wicked and cruel man. Lead students in a discussion of Digory's attitude toward his uncle. When is one excused from obeying and adult because of the nature of their actions? Have students find Scripture to support their views. Give them reference points to help them clearly know when it is OK to disobey someone who is leading them to do that which is wrong in God's sight.

3. Have students write a journal entry as if they are Polly or Digory writing about their experience in coming to the Wood Between the Worlds.

VOCABULARY CHAPTERS 2-3

queer:	(adj)	differing from the usual or normal; peculiar; strange
asylum:	(n)	an institution for the care of the needy or sick and especially of the insane
profound:	(adj)	marked by intellectual depth or insight
sages:	(n)	one who is distinguished for wisdom
destiny:	(n)	a predetermined course of events
grave:	(adj)	dignified; solemn
noble:	(adj)	of a superior nature
charwoman:	(adj)	a cleaning woman especially in large buildings
preposterous:	(adj)	contrary to nature or reason; absurd
adept:	(n)	expert
chivalry:	(n)	the spirit or character of the ideal knight
vague:	(adj)	not clear, definite, or distinct
gassing	(v)	*Slang* To talk excessively

QUESTIONS CHAPTERS 2-3

1. What threat did Uncle Andrew use to keep Digory from screaming? Who was he really concerned about?

2. Who was Mrs. Lefay?

3. What did she leave in Uncle Andrew's care?

4. What instructions did she give to him that he did not follow?

5. Why does Uncle Andrew say Mrs. Lefay was a remarkable woman?

6. According to Uncle Andrew, what kind of writing was on the box?

7. What was actually in the box? Where does Uncle Andrew say it came from?

8. When Uncle Andrew talks about what has happened to the guinea pigs he has used, what does he reveal about the kind of person he is?

9. What does he believe about the rings he has made?

10. When Uncle Andrew tells Digory he should go and rescue Polly or she could be facing all kinds of dangers, what does Digory tell Uncle Andrew he is?

11. When Digory reaches the other world, from what does he emerge? What is unusual about his condition?

12. When he finds Polly, how long does she say she has been in this place?

13. How do Polly and Digory remember what has happened to them?

14. Why does Polly not want to stay longer where they are?

15. When they first try to jump into the pool, what happens? Why?

16. What does Polly suggest as a name for the place where they are now?

17. What does Digory suggest they do?

18. What does Polly want assurance of first? At what compromise do they arrive?

19. When they first try to jump into another pool, what happens? Why?
20. What is the truth about the rings?

ANSWERS TO QUESTIONS CHAPTERS 2-3

1. He implies that if Digory's mother hears him screaming, it could cause her irreparable harm. Of course, his concern is actually for himself. He does not want the other adults in the household to discover what he is doing.

2. Mrs. Lefay was Uncle Andrew's godmother, who apparently was a rather peculiar and eccentric old woman, as well as being a criminal. She had spent the last part of her life in prison.

3. She left a box in his care.

4. She instructed him to burn it after her death, following specific ceremonies.

5. Uncle Andrew says that she was one of the last mortals in England to have fairy blood in her, making him one of the last men to actually have a fairy godmother.

6. Atlantian

7. There was dust in the box, which Uncle Andrew believes came from Atlantis.

8. He is a cruel, uncaring person. He has no feelings for the living things he has used in his experiments. He only cares for himself and what he feels he can accomplish.

9. He believes the yellow rings will take a person to another world, and the green rings will bring the person back to this world.

10. a coward

11. He emerges from a pool of water, but he is completely dry. Neither he nor his clothes are wet at all.

12. She says she has always been in this place.

13. When they see the guinea pig with the yellow ring tied to it, they both remember Uncle Andrew and how he sent the guinea pig, as well as both of them, to this place.

14. She fears they will fall asleep here and will sleep forever and ever.

15. When they jump in, they find the water is only ankle deep. They still have on their yellow rings, which keep them from leaving the place they are now.

16. The Wood Between the Worlds

17. Digory suggests they explore some of the other pools. He wants to see if they lead to other worlds besides their own.

18. Polly wants to make sure they can return to their own world, so they agree to return part of the way back, then change rings when they are sure they can make it back, but before they are actually back in Uncle Andrew's laboratory.

19. They experience the same thing they had experienced the first time they tried to jump into the pool leading back to earth. The water is only ankle deep. This time it is because they have on the yellow rings, believing the yellow rings are for the "outward journey, while the green ones are for the return journey. This was what Uncle Andrew had believed.

20. They discover that the yellow rings draw one back to the Wood Between the World, while the green rings repel one away from the place, regardless of what world one is reaching.

CHAPTER 4

After changing the rings to green and jumping into the pool again, the magic succeeds in transporting the children, first through a mass of darkness and vague shapes, then through growing light until they find themselves standing on solid ground. They find themselves in a strange place with a strange light, and Polly is uneasy. She immediately declares her dislike for the place. The light is dull, red and steady, and the sky is dark; a blue that is almost black. Digory wonders if they have arrived as a thunderstorm is about to begin, or maybe an eclipse. For no particular reason, they are both talking in whispers, and continue to hold each other's hands. They are standing in some sort of courtyard with high walls in which there are windows that have no glass in them. The stone with which everything is built seems to be red, although that may be a reflection from the sun. It is obvious that the place is ancient. The corners of all the stones are worn until they are round, and one of the doorways is piled with rubble. They turn around in circles, fearful someone peering from one of the windows will see them. Digory asks if Polly thinks anyone lives here, to which she replies no, they have not heard a sound since they came. Digory wants to stand and listen. They find the silence here different from the silence in the Wood Between the Worlds. There the silence is rich and warm; here it is cold and dead. Polly begs to return home, but Digory persists in his desire to explore the place. When he mentions being afraid, Polly rises to the challenge, dropping his hand and declaring she will go anywhere he will. They put their green rings into their right pockets, and Digory reminds Polly the yellow ones are in their left pockets. They can return to the Wood Between the World anytime they want simply by touching the yellow rings. As they enter the doorway, it is apparent these buildings have not been used for hundreds, or possibly thousands, of years. Polly is again apprehensive about the safety of exploring such precarious surroundings. Digory, however, says that if they have lasted this long they will last a little longer, but they should whisper so their voices will not cause the walls to collapse. They continue to go from one courtyard into another, amazed by the immensity of the rooms and the statues they are seeing. The people who lived here must have been magnificent. There are not even any ants or spiders living. Everything seems to be dead. Digory has just about decided they should put on their rings and return to the Wood Between the Worlds when they find some immense metal doors which look like they might have been gold. When they open the door, they find the room populated with people wearing magnificently colorful clothing. Each of the figures is robed and wearing a crown on his or her head. Their robes are crimson, silvery grey, dark purple and vivid green with patterns of flowers and beasts on them. There are precious stones on their crowns and hanging from chains around their necks. Polly is amazed, wondering why their clothing has not deteriorated. Digory, on the other hand, knows the answer immediately. He senses the magic in the room, and asks Polly if she can't feel it as well. While Polly is admiring the clothing, Digory is examining the faces of the figures, and declares that these were nice people. Polly agrees, believing the faces look kind and wise. However, as they go farther, the faces look more solemn. Farther into the room, they find the faces look cruel and not at all happy. They believe these people have done things that are dreadful, and have suffered dreadful things. Although all of the figures are taller than people of our world, the last figure is tallest of all. She is also beautiful, and very fierce looking. When Digory was an old man, he said he had never seen a woman so beautiful, although Polly did not share his view. Beyond the woman are a number of empty chairs, as if waiting for other occupants. In the middle of the room is a square pillar holding a golden arch from which there hangs a golden bell, and a little golden hammer with which to hit the bell. As Digory stoops to examine the table, Polly notices writing on it. Neither think they will be able to read it, but as they look, the letters magically transform into a language they can read. It contains a verse which reads: "Make your choice, adventurous Stranger/Strike the bell and bide the danger,/Or wonder, till it drives you mad,/What would have followed if you had." Seeing the word "danger,"

Polly immediately votes against the idea, but Digory is fascinated and can't stand walking away without finding out what will happen if they strike the bell. As they argue, Digory reveals he feels the magic working on him, and feels compelled to strike the bell, while Polly feels it is an unwise action. As Polly is about to reach for her ring and leave him, Digory grabs her wrist with one hand, and strikes the bell with the other. Polly is crying with anger, but soon forgets it as the sound of the bell becomes louder and louder. Just as it seems the waves of the bell will begin to die down, there is a sound "like the roar of a distant train, then like the crash of a falling tree." Finally everything becomes quiet, but the walls around them begin to crumble and fall. Polly says, "There! I hope you're satisfied!" To which Digory replies, "Well, it's over, anyway." However, they find they could not be more wrong.

SUGGESTED ACTIVITIES CHAPTER 4

1. Have students illustrate the world found by Digory and Polly, particularly the hall of the Kings and Queens.

2. Discuss imagery: the use of words to appeal to the senses, and the way in which Lewis uses imagery in this chapter. (darkness/light/various shades of light; the sound of the bell). Ask students to write a short story using descriptive terms that appeal to the senses.

3. Discuss the temptation faced by Digory, as well as temptation in general. Why is it so difficult to walk away from temptation? Why was Polly able to refuse to be drawn into the desire to ring the bell, while Digory could not resist?

VOCABULARY CHAPTER 4

eclipse:	(n)	the total or partial obscuring of one heavenly body by another
pillared:	(adj)	having strong upright supports
rubble:	(n)	broken fragments especially of a destroyed building
enchantments:	(n)	magical spells
avalanche:	(n)	a mass of snow, ice, earth, or rock sliding down a mountainside
despairing:	(adj)	hopeless
obstinate:	(adj)	fixed and unyielding (as in an opinion or course) despite reason or persuasion; stubborn

The Magician's Nephew

QUESTIONS CHAPTER 4

1. What is the difference in the way that Digory and Polly react to the new world in which they find themselves?

2. What is strange about the light?

3. How does Digory describe the weather?

4. As the children survey their surroundings, what do they fear?

5. What is Polly's conclusion about the condition of the place?

6. What is the conflict between Polly and Digory?

7. When they see the wall bulging outward in one place, looking like it might fall into the courtyard, how does each of the children react?

8. From their reactions so far, what do you know about Digory's and Polly's personalities?

9. What do they find that causes excitement for both of the children?

10. What causes more interest for Polly in this room?

11. What practical question does Polly bring up?

12. How does Digory's answer indicate that he is being influenced by their surroundings?

13. As they study the people in the room, what conclusion do they draw?

14. What is special about the last figure?

15. What do they discover in the middle of the room?

16. What is unusual about the writing on the pillar?

17. How does Digory react to the writing? What is Polly's response?

18. As they struggle over the issue, what does Polly observe about Digory?

19. What is the result of giving in to temptation?

20. When Digory rings the bell, what is the consequence?

ANSWERS TO QUESTIONS CHAPTER 4

1. Digory merely observes what a strange place it is, but seems enthralled, while Polly immediately announces she does not like the place.

2. The light is like no other light they have ever seen. It is a dull, reddish light, and does not seem to be coming from a candle or an electric light or a lamp. It is a steady light with no flickering, and no cheerful qualities to it.

3. He says it seems a thunderstorm or an eclipse is about to occur.

4. They are afraid someone might be watching them from one of the windows.

5. She believes no one is living here – it is all ruins.

6. Polly wants to go home, but Digory wants to stay and explore the world.

7. Polly observes that the wall doesn't look very safe, while Digory says that if it has stayed up this long, it will stay up a little longer.

8. Polly tends to be the more cautious of the two, while Digory is more curious and willing to take risks in order to investigate what is behind the next barrier.

9. They finally find a room in which there are what appears to be hundreds of people, all seated, in luxurious, brightly colored clothing. They seem to be wax figures, since none of them are moving, and they all have the appearance of royalty.

10. Polly is entranced with the clothing the people are wearing.

11. She wonders why their clothing has not rotted away.

12. He tells Polly it is magic, asking her if she has not felt the power of the magic in the room.

13. The first people seem to be very kind and wise looking. As the figures progress, they become more solemn and then begin to become cruel. While the figures in the middle of the room were strong and proud and happy, the figures at the end of the room were merely cruel. It seemed they had done things that were dreadful and had had dreadful things done to them.

14. The last figure is the most interesting. She is the tallest, the most beautiful and the most richly dressed of all of the figures. She also has a fierceness and pride about her face that is frightening.

15. There is a square pillar holding a small bell with a small hammer. There is also writing on the pillar.

16. Although it is logical they will not be able to read writing on the pillar in this strange world, the letters seem to transform so that, as they look at it, they are able to read the inscription.

17. Digory is immediately challenged – he feels tempted to ring the bell. Polly, on the other hand, feels the warning of the message and wants the leave the bell alone and leave this world.

18. He is becoming like his uncle.

19. Giving in to temptation leads to sin, which ultimately leads to destruction.

20. The bell rings with an intensity that grows louder and louder until the roof falls in and the walls fall around them.

CHAPTERS 5-6

As the children watch, the robed figure Digory thought was so beautiful rises from her chair. The children immediately realize she is a great queen. As she surveys the damage done to the building, they are unsure how she will feel about what has happened. She demands to know who has awakened her; who has broken the spell. When Digory admits it was he, she does not believe that could be true, since he is merely a child. Polly tells her they came from another world under a magic spell. The Queen asks Digory if this is true, continuing to ignore Polly, much to her chagrin. She concludes that Digory is not a magician and therefore must be a magician's servant. He must have traveled here under the power of another. He admits to her it was his Uncle Andrew. As they are talking, the room is continuing to fall around them. The Queen speaks calmly, holding out a hand to each of the children and telling them they cannot stay here or they will be buried under the ruins. Polly thinks the woman is terrible, but her strength is great, and she cannot reach the yellow ring while her hand is held by the Queen. She wishes she can get Digory alone to speak to him. As the Queen leads them out of the palace, they hear the structure collapsing behind them. Digory is thinking what a brave and strong woman the Queen is; hoping she will share with them the story of this place. As they go along, she points out doors to dungeons, torture chambers and other places of death and punishment. Finally they come to the main entrance, where there are enormous doors with bars too high for them to reach. The Queen lets go of their hands, recites some words and gestures with her hands. The doors crumble until there is nothing left of them. Digory is amazed, and the Queen asks if his uncle has that kind of power. Not waiting for his answer, she tells him she will find out later, then warns that is what happens to those who stand in her way. As they exit the palace, they see a dying sun in the sky along with a single star. Spread out before them is a vast, deserted city as far as their eyes can see. The Queen tells them this was the city of Charn, the city of the King of Kings. She asks if Digory's uncle rules over a city as great as this. Digory is a about to explain he does not rule over any cities when she silences him and begins to reminisce about the past of the city when it was a living, thriving city. She explains to the children that she, Jadis, had ended the world, but blames it on her sister. They had been at war with each other. There was a magical word known to the ancient kings of the land which would destroy all living things except the one who spoke it. When her sister had destroyed all of Jadis's army and believed she had the victory, Jadis used the magical word against her. Polly asks about all of the common people, and Digory also commiserates with her. Jadis tells them the common people were her people. She was Queen and was free from all rules. Digory remembers his Uncle Andrew using similar words. Digory asks if the Deplorable Word is what made the sun so small and red and cold in this world. When he explains their world has a sun that is smaller and warmer and Jadis realizes they live in a younger world, she has a look of greed like that the children have seen on Uncle Andrew's face. She immediately announces she will go with them to their world. They are aghast. Polly did not like her to begin with, and Digory has had enough of her. She believes they were sent to bring her to their world. She announces she will go and rule their world, but Digory tells her they will not let her. She replies that many great kings thought they could stand before the House of Charn, but they all fell. If Digory is fearful for his uncle, she will see he keeps his life and throne if he honors her. She asks if he is king of the whole world or only part, to which Digory replies he is not king of anywhere. Jadis believes he must be lying; a common man cannot be a magician. She believes he must have seen her great beauty and sent the children to fetch her. Digory replies "Not exactly" Polly says, "It's absolute bosh" The Queen grabs Polly's hair, Digory shouts "Now!" and they grab their rings and rush upward toward the green light.

As they emerge from the pool, Polly is yelling, "Let go! Let go!" Digory tells her he is not touching her, but they quickly discover Jadis still has Polly by the hair. They have discovered another property of the magical rings – one does not have to touch the rings, but only someone touching the ring. Seeing her in the Wood, Jadis looks much paler, and neither child is intimidated by her. They both demand she let go of Polly, then struggle with her. Polly urges Digory to quickly put on their green rings and go home, but Jadis pleads with them not to leave her there. Digory feels sorry for her, but Polly rightly tells him she is not sincere. As they jump into the pool, Digory feels a cold finger and thumb on his ear. They emerge in Uncle Andrew's laboratory with Uncle Andrew staring in awe at the Witch they have brought with them. On Earth, Jadis seemed even larger than she had before. As a matter of fact, it has been told that those of Charn have the blood of giants running through their veins. She also looks more fierce and frightening than before. As Polly looks at Uncle Andrew bowing and scraping before Jadis, she concludes he appears to be a "frightened little shrimp," but she also recognizes the common mark of magic that both Jadis and Andrew share. It is a look of wickedness that Jadis had not been able to find in Digory's face. After seeing the two together, the children know they will never again be afraid of Uncle Andrew. Jadis demands to know where the magician is who has called her from her world, and Andrew stammers trying to tell her it is he. Looking into his face, Jadis acknowledges Andrew is a magician "of a sort," but warns him not to speak to her as if they are equals. She surmises he is not of royal blood. Jadis informs Andrew his kind of magician was made an end of in her world a thousand years ago, but she will allow him to be her servant. Her first order is to obtain a chariot, or flying carpet, or dragon; whatever means of transport royals use in this world, and take her where she can get jewels and clothing so that she may begin her conquest of the world the next day. Andrew tells her he will find a cab, and the Witch warns him against any kind of treachery. The children are afraid she will bring up what happened in the Wood between the Worlds, but later conclude that she has no memory of it, and will never remember anything that happens there no matter how many times she goes there. Jadis does not seem to notice the children at all, and presently leaves the room in search of Andrew, wondering what is taking him so long. Polly tells Digory she must be getting home – it is getting late and she will be in trouble. Digory implores her to return soon, as they need to come up with some kind of plan, but she replies that is Uncle Andrew's problem now. Polly replies she is going home through the tunnel, and if he wants her to return, he should say he is sorry, but he does not know what he should be sorry for. Polly brings up his grabbing of her wrist, ringing of the bell, and turning back at the woods which allowed the witch to come home with them. Digory reluctantly agrees he owes her an apology, then Polly tells him she does not understand why he will be in trouble over Jadis. It is his uncle's problem now. Digory explains he is concerned about his mother, and what will happen if Jadis happens into his mother's room and frightens her. Uncle Andrew, meanwhile, was trying on clothes in order to find the most impressive outfit to wear before the Witch. After taking two drinks to calm his nerves, he began to believe she might actually fall in love with him. He goes downstairs, finds his sister and asks to borrow five pounds from her. She promptly refuses, to which he responds he needs the money to entertain a distinguished visitor who has just arrived. Aunt Letty informs him the doorbell has not rung. At that moment, the door is flung open and the Witch stands before her with her arms bare and her eyes flashing.

SUGGESTED ACTIVITIES CHAPTERS 5-6

1. Ask students to illustrate one of the scenes in this section: the children coming through the pool with Jadis holding Digory's ear, Jadis meeting Uncle Andrew for the first time, or Jadis standing before Uncle Andrew and Aunt Letty.

2. Have students write a skit and act out their version of this section.

3. Ask students to research the clothing and the transportation of this time period, and report on it, contrasting it with that of today.

VOCABULARY CHAPTERS 5-6

sulky:	(adj)	morose; moody
bosh:	(n)	foolish talk or action: nonsense
minion:	(n)	a servile dependent, follower, or underling
shamming:	(v)	pretending
procure	(v)	to get possession of; obtain
treachery:	(n)	violation of allegiance or trust
pax:	(n)	peace
homely:	(adj)	familiar
frockcoat:	(n)	an outer garment worn especially by men
hansom:	(n)	a 2-wheeled covered carriage with the driver's seat elevated at the rear
deucedly:	(adv)	devilish; excessive; extreme

QUESTIONS CHAPTERS 5-6

1. What has been the result of the ringing bell?

2. When Digory tells the Queen he has awakened her, what is her response?

3. How does she respond differently to Polly and Digory?

4. How does she know Digory is not a magician? What is he lacking?

5. As the Queen takes the children's hands, what is the difference in the way they react to her?

6. As she points out parts of the palace, what is the general theme of the rooms she shows them? What does this tell you about her?

7. What problem seems to face them when they reach the doors of the palace?

8. How does the Queen solve this problem?

9. When Jadis tells them who destroyed this world, whose fault does she say it was?

10. What does Jadis say that is something Uncle Andrew has said?

11. What happens when Jadis realizes the children come from a world that is younger?

12. What does Jadis plan to do when she reaches their world?

13. When Digory and Polly emerge from the pool into the Wood Between the Worlds this time, what do they learn about the rings that Uncle Andrew did not know?

14. How is Jadis different in the Wood Between the Worlds than she was in Charn?

15. When the children see Uncle Andrew next to Jadis, how do they respond?

16. What does Jadis think of Uncle Andrew? What does she tell him he can be to her?

17. What does Jadis send Andrew to get?

18. What is Digory most fearful of?

19. As Andrew gets ready to go out, of what does he convince himself?

20. What does Andrew tell his sister? Does she believe him? What surprises her?

ANSWERS TO QUESTIONS CHAPTERS 5-6

1. One of the figures; the one Digory thought was so beautiful, has come to life.

2. She tells him he is a common child, and it is apparent he has no royal or noble blood in his veins. She asks how he dares to come into her house.

3. Although she is indignant that Digory is the one who has awakened her, she ignores Polly entirely, and only speaks to her through Digory.

4. When she looks into Digory's face she knows he is not a magician because he does not have the mark of a magician.

5. Polly thinks she is a terrible woman, and hopes Digory will keep quiet and not let her find out about the rings. Digory, on the other hand, thinks the woman is brave and strong, and is hoping she will tell them the story of the place.

6. They are all places of death and torture, which indicate that the woman's interest is in death and punishment. She is a woman of a fierce, angry, warlike nature who revels in that which is normally seen as negative.

7. The doors were fastened with bars that were too high up for any of them to reach.

8. She stretches out her hands, and opens them with magic.

9. She tells them she destroyed the world, but that it was her sister's fault.

10. She says she is free from all rules; the rules that apply to other people do not apply to great queens because they have the weight of the world on their shoulders. Uncle Andrew had said the rules that applied to others did not apply to him because he was a magician.

11. She immediately decides she wants to go to their world.

12. She plans to take over their world and rule it.

13. It is not necessary to touch the rings in order to be transported by them. It is only necessary to touch someone who is touching a ring.

14. She is paler, and she seems to be much weaker. She appeals to the children for mercy as they plan to leave her there.

15. They are no longer afraid of Uncle Andrew, and compare him to a shrimp.

16. She tells him she can see he is not of royal blood, but is a magician who works by rules and books. She tells him he can be her servant.

17. She sends him to find her some transportation: a chariot, a dragon, a flying carpet, or whatever is used for transportation in this world.

18. He is fearful Jadis will go into his mother's room and scare her to death.

19. He convinces himself the Witch might be falling in love with him.

20. Andrew tells his sister there is a distinguished visitor from a foreign land, but she does not believe him because the doorbell has not rung. She is surprised when Jadis shows up in the room.

CHAPTERS 7-8

As the Witch shrieks out demands for her chariot, Uncle Andrew quickly loses all thoughts of her falling in love with him, and cowers before her. Aunt Letty rises from her knees and demands to know who this person is. As Andrew mutters incoherently about a very important foreigner, Aunt Letty indignantly issues an ultimatum that she is to leave the house or she will call for the police, believing Jadis must be someone from a circus. The conflict between the two women becomes more heated, as Jadis is insulted, draws herself to her full height and threatens to blast Letty if she does not go down on her knees. When Letty refuses, Jadis makes the same gesture and horrible sounding words she did in Charn. However, instead of turning Letty to dust, her magic has no effect here. Letty concludes the woman is drunk at the same time Jadis realizes her magic has no power in this world. However, Jadis still has the advantage when it comes to size, so she grabs Letty by the neck, raises her off the floor, and throws her across the room. At that precise moment, the maid appears to announce the hansom has arrived at the door. Uncle Andrew makes some semblance of a protest against way Jadis has abused his sister, but Jadis quickly silences him. Digory quickly realizes the seriousness of having Jadis loosed on London, but his attention is distracted by the housemaid calling him to look after his aunt. Aunt Letty has received only a few bruises and quickly regains control of the situation. She sends the maid to the police station to report there is a lunatic at large, then takes lunch to Digory's mother. Digory is most concerned for his mother, and does not want to have Jadis at large in their house. He does not know she has lost any of her powers in coming into this world, and can imagine her using her powers to take over the world. He tries to strategize how to get her to touch him so he can touch the yellow ring and take her back to the Wood Between the World. He also wonders if she will find herself weak if he can get her to that place. In the end, not knowing where to look for her, he decides the only thing to do is to wait for Jadis and Uncle Andrew to come back to their house. As he waits, Digory wonders what Polly is doing. Meanwhile, Polly has returned home late for dinner with her shoes and stockings very wet. When her parents question her and find she was with Digory Kirke and her feet got wet in a pool in a wood, her parents conclude Polly has gone off somewhere without their permission, so she was told she would not be allowed to play with Digory anymore, and was sent to bed for two soldi hours. As he is waiting, Digory hears a woman come with grapes for his mother, and Aunt Letty tells the woman it would take grapes from the land of youth to help Digory's mother now. Nothing from this world will be able to help her. It occurs to Digory that there are other worlds. He has experienced them, and maybe he can find something that will cure his mother. He considers putting on the yellow ring and going back to search through all of the worlds until he finds something to help his mother, when he hears a fire engine, and realizes it is coming to his house. He also suddenly comprehends it is Jadis who is bringing the fire engine toward the house. The hansom is coming toward the house without a driver, but with Jadis standing on the roof, whipping the horse until it is worked up into a lather, and frightened almost to death. It gallops to the front door, barely missing the lamp-post, rears up on it hind legs, then crashes into the lam-post and breaks it into several pieces. The Witch jumps clear and onto the horse's back, and begins to whisper things into the horse's ear. This stirs the horse up even more, and it rears on its hind legs, screaming and neighing. Soon a second hansom appears with a policeman, followed by a crowd of people. An old gentleman emerges from the wreck of the hansom, and Digory guesses it is Uncle Andrew. A large man rushes up, accusing Jadis of stealing jewels from his shop and urging the policeman to arrest her. This is followed by others who have been robbed, all demanding the same satisfaction, and one mentioning to make sure Uncle Andrew is arrested as well. Digory has been watching the agitated horse's flying hoofs, biding his time and waiting for an opportunity to make a dash for the Witch and touch her while simultaneously touching his yellow ring. Meanwhile, the cabby has arrived, appealing his case to the policeman. Overwhelmed, the police officer tells the cabby he will have to take his place in line like all the rest, but the cabby replies there is no time for that. The horse is descended from a cavalry horse, and if he continues to be provoked, there will be murder before it is all finished. The policeman gratefully backs away, allowing the cabby to move in toward the wildly thrashing horse. As he tries to calm Strawberry, the horse, the cabby speaks in the same calm voice to the Witch, suggesting she might be more satisfied at home lying down with a cup of tea. Jadis looks at him and says, "Dog, unhand our royal charger. We are the Empress Jadis."

This declaration from Jadis brings about a cheer from the crowd, and she bows slightly to them, then realizes they are ridiculing her as they all begin to laugh. Although she has lost her ability to use magic, she has not lost her terrible strength, and she proves it by wrenching off one of the cross bars of the lamp-post as if it is a mere stick. She tosses the metal bar into the air and catches it, brandishing her new weapon and urging the horse forward. Digory realizes this is his chance, then hears a voice beside him saying, "Quick, Digory. This must be stopped." Polly has joined him, leaving her house the moment she was allowed out of bed. Digory is thankful for Polly's help, and asks her to manage the ring while holding onto him. Before he can get to the Witch, she has already knocked out one policeman. A second one is down and the military is being called as Digory tries to find his way to her. The cabby proves the bravest in the crowd, holding onto the horse and trying to calm him. Finally Digory grabs the Witch's ankle, but is kicked off before he can shout to Polly. The crowd begins to throw stones, and Jadis threatens to destroy their world as she destroyed Charn. Finally he grabs her ankle and holds on. He can hear Uncle Andrew's voice from somewhere, but shouts to Polly to "Go!" When they emerge in the Wood Between the Worlds, they find they have brought not only Jadis, but also Uncle Andrew, the cabby and the horse Strawberry. Jadis becomes pale and sickly, dropping her face into the horse's mane. Uncle Andrew is shivering, but Strawberry has calmed and is looking much better. He crosses over and begins to drink from one of the pools. They are all still touching each other, so Polly yells, "Quick, Greens!" Before Strawberry can get his drink, they all sink into darkness, and emerge on dry land. The only thing is, it is completely dark. As they wonder where they are, Digory wonders if they have re-entered Charn in the middle of the night. Jadis replies they are not in Charn, but in an empty world where there is nothing. There are no stars in the sky, and it is so dark they cannot even see each other. They can feel something like earth under their feet, but there is no grass or wood, and there is no wind and the air is cold and dry. The Witch announces her doom has come upon her, to which Andrew protests things can't be that bad, appealing to the cabby for a drink of something alcoholic. The cabby declares that if they are all intact and no one has any broken bones, the best thing they can do is sing a hymn, which he proceeds to do. The children join in the singing, but Andrew and Jadis do not. Toward the end of the song, Digory feels someone plucking at his elbow and concludes it must be Uncle Andrew due to the smell of alcohol and tobacco. Uncle Andrew whispers for him to slip on his ring, but Jadis has excellent hearing, and warns him she will not tolerate any treachery. Digory replies he would not be such a pig as to leave Polly and the cabby and the horse, anyway. Suddenly in the darkness they begin to hear something. A voice has begun to sing, and it is the most beautiful singing they have ever heard. The horse hears it, too, and it is obvious he likes it. Suddenly the voice is joined by thousands of other voices, all in harmony with it. At the same time, the sky overhead is blazing with stars. Digory is certain the stars themselves are singing, and that it is the First Voice that has made them sing. The Cabby declares he would have been a better man all his life if he had known there were things like this. As the Voice on the earth becomes louder, the voices in the sky become softer, and the sky begins to turn grey. As the light begins to encompass them, they can see one another's faces. The Cabby and the children are filled with joy and wonder, and their eyes are shining. Uncle Andrew's mouth is open, but there is no joy in his eyes. It is obvious he doe not like the Voice. The Witch seems to understand the Voice better than any of them. Her lips are pressed tightly shut, and her fists are clenched. She hates this world. She wants to destroy this world and the magic that is in it. The horse seems more alive and energetic. It is possible to believe his father was in battles. The eastern sky changes from white to pink to gold, and the air begins to shake as the Voice rises. As the Voice swells the most glorious sound, the sun rises. Just as the sun in Charn was older than ours, the sun in this world is younger than ours. It gives the appearance of laughing for joy as it rises. Finally the singer Himself becomes visible. He is a Lion. The Witch declares this is a terrible world, and they must fly at once. Uncle Andrew agrees, adding that if he were younger and had a gun... The Cabby asks Andrew if he thinks he would be able to shoot him. Jadis demands Andrew to prepare the magic, and he says he must have both children touching him, then orders Digory to put on his Homeward ring, hoping to escape without the Witch. However, Jadis tries to get her hands into Digory's pockets and grab the rings. Digory, however, grabs Polly and jumps away, declaring they will both vanish if either Andrew or Jadis come near. Apologizing to the Cabby, he tells Andrew and Jadis they should enjoy living together. He feels his obligation is to protect Polly and get her home. The Cabby warns them to be quiet. The song has changed.

SUGGESTED ACTIVITIES CHAPTERS 7-8

1. The children have observed the beginning of Narnia, but it is much like the creation account of Genesis. Ask students to write a short story in which they are transported back in time so that they are able to observe the actual beginning of our world as it is created by God. Have them describe what it is like as if they are actually there observing it, just as Digory and Polly were observing the creation of Narnia.

2. Have students compare/contrast Lewis's account of the creation of Narnia with God's account of the creation of earth in Genesis. In what ways are they similar? How are they different?

3. Since this chapter involves riot control as well as situations that would be handled, in our day, by a SWAT unit, tour a police station and have the policemen explain how they handle hostage situations and situations where there are crowds out of control and human lives are in danger.

VOCABULARY CHAPTERS 7-8

hussy:	(n)	a lewd or brazen woman
sal volatile:	(n)	a solution of ammonium carbonate in alcohol or ammonia water, used in smelling salts
lunatic:	(n)	an insane person
rampaging:	(v)	to rush about wildly
throttle:	(v)	choke; strangle
flogging:	(v)	to beat with or as if with a rod or whip
impertinent:	(adj)	rude; insolent

Novel Insights Plus

QUESTIONS CHAPTERS 7-8

1. How does the presence of the Witch change Uncle Andrew's thoughts about her?

2. How is Aunt Letty's response more like Polly's response to her?

3. From Aunt Letty's encounter with Jadis, what do you know about her character?

4. What does Jadis discover about her power?

5. What is Digory's biggest problem? What knowledge does he not have?

6. What happened to Polly after she returned home?

7. What does Digory overhear while he is waiting for his uncle and Jadis to return?

8. Why does this give him hope now, while it might not have before?

9. Read Heb. 11:1. How is Digory's experience like this?

10. What happens that interrupts Digory's thoughts?

11. What impact has Jadis had on those with whom she has come in contact?

12. What is she being accused of doing?

13. What is Digory's plan of action? What is his greatest obstacle?

14. When the Cabby tries to calm his horse, what announcement does Jadis make?

15. How is this received by the people? What does Jadis do in response to their reaction?

16. Just as Digory is about to make his move, who shows up to help him?

17. When they emerge in the Wood Between the Worlds, who have they brought with them this time?

18. What does Strawberry decide to do? How does this affect everyone else?

19. In the world where they emerge this time, what is different?

20. What does Digory think at first? What does the Witch tell him?

21. What suggestion does the Cabby make? Who joins him?

22. What does Uncle Andrew try to get Digory to do? What is Digory's response?

23. How does the music they hear affect each of the characters differently, including the horse?

24. As they observe, what takes place in this world?

25. Who is the one making the music?

ANSWERS TO QUESTIONS CHAPTERS 7-8

1. He is no longer thinking of her in terms of her falling in love with him, but is cowering in fear of her.

2. Aunt Letty is not afraid of her, but orders her out of the house. Like Polly, she sees her immediately as a source of evil and wants to escape from her. The two males are blinded by her beauty and unable to see the fierceness and danger of her evil.

3. Aunt Letty is apparently a very brave woman of upright character; one who prefers doing what is right regardless of the consequences to her own safety.

4. On earth, she no longer has the power to reduce people and things to dust by merely pointing and reciting an incantation. In short, she has lost her magical powers.

5. Digory's biggest problem is his fear that Jadis will start "rampaging" around the house and will frighten his mother, causing her to have a heart attack and die. He knows beyond all else he must protect his mother from this woman. He does not have the knowledge that Jadis does not have her magical powers in this world.

6. Polly was punished because she came home with wet shoes and stockings, and her parents believe she has gone somewhere with Digory that she was not allowed to go. She was given only those parts of her dinner that were not good to eat, and sent to her bed for two hours.

7. He overhears his aunt saying that the only thing that would help his mother would be to have some fruit from the "land of youth."

8. Before, he would not have believed such a place existed, but now he has seen for himself that there are different worlds that exist outside our own, some of which contain powerful magic that he could never have imagined before.

9. Faith is believing in that which we cannot see, but trust it is true because we believe in God. Digory has faith in the "land of youth" now because he has seen that there are things outside his experience that he cannot understand.

10. A commotion outside the house, indicating Jadis has returned.

11. She has caused a riot throughout the town, stirring up people everywhere she has gone, and they have all followed her back to Uncle Andrew's house.

12. She has stolen from several retailers, particularly a jeweler. The jeweler and a number of errand boys are following the hansom driven by the Witch, trying to recover their stolen goods.

13. Digory plans to jump in and grab the Witch as soon as possible while touching his yellow ring at the same time. The biggest problem he faces is the horse, which keeps raring up and turning around, making it dangerous for him to attempt to make the approach.

14. She declares that she is the "Empress Jadis."

15. The people begin to laugh and ridicule her, and Jadis grabs one of the cross-bars from the lamp-post, wrenching it from the lamp-post and brandishing it like a weapon. She uses it to bash two policemen over the head.

16. Polly

17. Of course, they intended to bring the Witch. However, they have also unwittingly brought Uncle Andrew, the Cabby and the horse.

18. He decides to drink from one of the pools, causing the children to put on their green rings and jump into the pool, taking the entire entourage into the pool.

19. This world is in complete darkness. There is no light at all.

20. Digory thinks they may have emerged in Charn in the middle of the night, but the Witch tells him this is not Charn, but an empty world in which nothing exists.

21. He suggests they should sing a hymn. Both of the children join him in singing.

22. He tries to get Digory to stand next to him, put on his ring and take the two of them back to London. Digory refuses, telling him that if he is going to take anyone back, he will take Polly back and leave the others there.

23. Digory, Polly and the Cabby are enthralled by the music, and it causes them feelings of great joy. The horse seems to be energized and is feeling like he is a young foal again. Both the Witch and Uncle Andrew find the Voice they hear frightening and something to be hated, rather than something to bring them joy.

24. Stars begin to appear in the sky, and the song being sung begins to become more and more triumphant, bringing about more and more light. As the light grows steadily brighter, they are able to see the shapes of hills against the sky. Soon the sun begins to rise, and they see a river flowing eastward towards the sun. The earth begins to take on more colors, and they see the Singer himself.

25. A Lion

CHAPTER 9

The children watch in fascination as the Lion paces about, changing the tone and the rhythm of his song. With every change, something new appears and spreads from the Lion like a pool. First there is grass; then small, spiky things which Digory finally identifies as trees begin to appear. Digory has difficulty enjoying the spectacle because Uncle Andrew continues to try to get close enough to him to pick his pocket. Of course, Uncle Andrew still believes the green rings are the "homeward" rings, and does not understand the true nature of the rings, but Digory does not want to lose either of them. Finally the Witch orders Andrew to stand back, threatening to use the lamp-post bar to bash out his brains if he tries to steal Digory and sneak back to his own world. Andrew becomes angry and spills the truth of what happened while he and the Witch were in London. She not only stole from the jeweler, but forced him to pawn his watch and chain in order to buy her an expensive lunch. As he goes on with his tirade, the Cabby silences him, telling him the thing to do at the present is to watch and listen. They are beginning to see full grown plants now, and Polly believes she sees the connection between the Lion's song and what is taking place. She feels she can "hear" the things the Lion is making up in the song, then see them become reality around them as they spring up on the landscape. Although it is all very invigorating, Digory and the Cabby are feeling uneasy as the Lion comes nearer and nearer. Uncle Andrew is visibly shaking, and his teeth are chattering. Suddenly the Witch walks straight ahead and flings the iron bar from the lamp-post at the Lion's head. She is only about twelve yards away; a distance from which it is impossible for her to miss. The bar hits the Lion between the eyes, glances off, and he continues to walk toward them as if nothing has happened. The Witch shrieks and runs, soon out of sight in the woods. Uncle Andrew tries to follow, but trips over a root and falls flat on his face into a little brook. The children are frozen, enthralled. The Lion continues his march, passing close enough to them that they could have touched him, but he pays them no attention. After he has passed, Uncle Andrew again attempts to persuade Digory to come close enough to him to help transport him back to their world. Digory warns him away, and commands Polly to stay close to him. As the two argue, Digory tells Andrew he wants to stay here and see what is going to happen, reminding his uncle he was the one who was curious about other worlds. Andrew bemoans his present state, and states he would probably enjoy this more if he were younger and had a gun. He mentions how extraordinarily delightful the air is in this place. The Cabby tells him he will go and see if he can give Strawberry a rubdown, admiring the horse's good sense. Uncle Andrew expresses his admiration for the Witch's courage in attacking the Lion with the iron bar, then calls to them to come and look at something. They are all amazed to see the iron bar has grown into a replica of the lamp-post, and it is lit. As they marvel over the growing lamp-post, Uncle Andrew notices how much younger he feels in this place, and makes plans for all the ways he can make money on this place, including bringing people here as a health resort. His first order of business, though, is to kill the Lion. At this, Polly likens him to the Witch – preoccupied with killing people. Andrew ignores her remarks and continues his revelry, musing at how long he might be able to live in this land where youth is renewed. He refers to it as "the land of youth." This clicks in Digory's mind, and he asks if there might be something here that would cure his mother. Andrew is distracted by his question, angrily replying that this is not a chemist's shop. Digory rebukes his uncle, since Mrs. Kirke is also Uncle Andrew's sister, and Digory thinks Andrew might care as much as he about her health. Digory resolves to go to the Lion himself and petition him on behalf of his mother. Andrew panics as Digory leaves, realizing the rings are now out of his reach. The Lion's tune has changed again, and is causing not only the humans, but the landscape to become agitated and unsettled. The earth begins to swell as humps appear and grow, and moles appear in the humps. Soon other animals begin to appear until Digory cannot hear the song of the Lion due to the noise of all of the animals. Although Digory cannot hear the Lion, he can see it. None of the animals seem to be afraid of the Lion, and Strawberry even trots past him and joins the other animals. The Lion is moving among the animals, touching his nose to two of them at a time. The animals he chooses follow him, while the others depart, their noises becoming less noticeable as they grow farther away. Finally only the chosen animals remain, and they all stand silently before the Lion. Digory also stands silently, knowing this is too important to interrupt even for this mother's health. He has to wait until this sacred moment is past. At last the Lion opens his mouth, and from the stars above come the words, "Narnia, Narnia, Narnia, awake. Love. Think. Speak. Be walking trees. Be talking beasts. Be divine waters."

SUGGESTED ACTIVITIES CHAPTER 9

1. Ask students to write their own song to represent the song sung by Aslan as he sings into being the world of Narnia.

2. Just as Digory is concerned about his mother who is ill, there are many in the hospital who could use someone who cares about their condition. Have students design cards to be delivered to children in the hospital and, if possible, take them to the patients themselves. If you personally know someone, have them adopt that person for this activity.

3. Assign a creative writing exercise in which students write an account of what has taken place in this chapter from the perspective of two of the characters, showing the difference in the way this episode would have been viewed by the different characters. (Students should not choose Digory and Polly, or the Witch and Uncle Andrew, but two characters who would present opposite perspectives).

VOCABULARY CHAPTER 9

abominably:	(adj)	odious; detestable; loathsome
civilities:	(n)	a polite act or expression
ostentatious:	(adj)	pretentious or excessive display
strab:	(adj)	a strap or an iron catch between the shaft and the harness on a drawn wagon, allowing the horse to stop or back up
sanitorium:	(n)	an institution for the treatment of chronic diseases or for medically supervised recuperation

QUESTIONS CHAPTER 9

1. How has the Lion's song changed?

2. What does the song accomplish? How does it change the look and feel of the landscape?

3. As the children are watching the new world coming to life, what happens to continually annoy Digory?

4. What misconception does Uncle Andrew have?

5. How does Jadis respond to his attempts?

6. What does Uncle Andrew reveal about the total extent of the Witch's actions while they were in London?

7. Who brings an end to their bickering?

8. As the Lion comes nearer, what does Polly discern about the song the Lion is singing?

9. As the Lion approaches, who is most frightened?

10. What does Jadis do? What is the outcome?

11. As the Lion passes closer to them, what do they notice about his reaction to them?

12. After the Lion has passed, what does Uncle Andrew try to get Digory to do again? What is Digory's response?

13. When Digory calls Polly over, what do they discover has happened to the bar from the lamp-post?

14. What possibilities immediately come to Uncle Andrew's mind when he sees the lamp-post?

15. What is the first thing he wants to do?

16. How does Uncle Andrew refer to the world in a way that strikes a chord with Digory?

17. What does Digory ask Uncle Andrew? What Uncle Andrew's response? How does this one exchange point out, again, the difference between Uncle Andrew and Digory?

18. What does Digory determine to do?

19. Imagery refers to using words that appeal to the senses. How does the author use imagery as he describes the animals emerging?

20. How has Strawberry changed?

21. What is the Lion doing among the animals?

22. What happens to the chosen animals?

23. When the Lion opens his mouth again, how is it different?

24. What begins to sing again?

25. From the declaration made by the Lion at the end of this chapter, what do you learn about this world?

ANSWERS TO QUESTIONS CHAPTER 9

1. It is softer and more lilting; a gentle, rippling music.

2. Foliage begins to spread out from the pool, covering the ground with soft green grass and causing trees to sprout up around them. The countryside now seems much warmer and softer than it did before, and the wind rustling through the plants can be seen. Having the different plants actually adds texture to the land as well.

3. Uncle Andrew continues to pester him, trying to get his hand into Digory's right pocket so that he can get hold of the green ring.

4. He still believes the green rings are "outward bound" rings, not understanding that the yellow rings were necessary to draw one back to the Wood Between the Worlds.

5. Jadis becomes angry, threatening him that if he comes within ten paces of the children she will knock his brains out.

6. She not only stole jewelry from the jeweler, but she forced Andrew to buy her such an expensive lunch that he had to pawn his watch, and chain in order to pay for her lunch. In addition to that, of course, she had assaulted the police and caused Andrew extreme embarrassment.

7. the Cabby

8. Polly begins to realize there is a relationship between the song the Lion is singing and the things that are being created in the world. She thinks the Lion is visualizing the things in his head, then singing each thing into being.

9. Uncle Andrew

10. She throws the metal bar from the lamp-post at the Lion, hitting him in the head, but the bar just bounces off his head.

11. Although he is close to them, he does not seem to notice them at all. He continues to sing his song, not smelling or snarling as they would expect a lion to do.

12. He tries to get Digory to use his ring to take him back home. Digory tells him to stay away; he is fascinated with the process that is occurring and wants to continue to watch. He reminds Uncle Andrew that he had been the one interested in learning about other worlds, and asks if he doesn't want to stay and learn something now that he is here.

13. The bar has grown into a complete, fully functional lamp-post, and is now taller than Digory.

14. He begins to think of all of the commercial possibilities of this world, both of "growing" scrap metal and of using the magical air of the place to develop a health resort where people can come and take advantage of the atmosphere – for a price.

15. The first thing he wants to do is kill the Lion.

16. He refers to it as "the land of youth."

17. Digory asks if there is anything here that would help his mother, and Andrew responds that this isn't a chemist's shop. Digory's concern is for his mother, while Andrew cares only for himself.

18. Digory determines to take his request to the Lion himself.

19. Examples of imagery: "grassy land bubbling like water in a pot," "showers of birds came out of trees," butterflies fluttered," and "the four baggy trouserer legs of an elephant" all appeal to the visual sense; "plop-plop," "there was so much cawing, cooing, braying, neighing, baying, barking, lowing, bleating and trumpeting" all appeal to the auditory sense.

20. Strawberry no longer seems like a tired, worn-out old cab horse. Instead, he is picking up his feet and holding his head erect as if the air here has totally transformed him into a younger, stronger horse.

21. The Lion is passing among the animals, touching two of them at a time with his nose.

22. Those he has chosen stand in a circle around him, while the other animals are sent away.

23. This time, instead of a song coming from his mouth, there is a long, warm breath that seems to sway the animals like the wind sways the trees.

24. The stars in the sky

25. The name of the world is Narnia; The trees here are able to walk; the animals are able to speak; the water here is divine.

CHAPTERS 10-11

The voice the children heard came from the Lion, and the result of what he said causes wild people to step out of the trees; gods and goddesses of the wood; Fauns and Satyrs and Dwarfs. In addition, there is a river god and his Naiad daughters. They all step forward and bow down to the Lion, saying, "Hail, Aslan. We hear and obey." Strawberry speaks up saying, "but we don't know very much yet." Polly is glad he has been chosen to be one of the speaking animals, and the Cabby admits he has always felt Strawberry was a very intelligent animal. Aslan speaks to the animals, admonishing them to be kind and gentle in their dealing with each other, then chooses a council to go with him and strategize how to deal with the enemy that is in their midst. He tells them that Narnia is not even five hours old, and an evil has already entered it. As the creatures on his council follow Aslan, the others try to discern what it was he was saying, misunderstanding what he said to be "a Neevil."

Digory explains to Polly that he must speak to Aslan and appeal to him for help for his mother. As they follow the animals, the animals try to determine exactly what the humans are. Finally they catch up to Strawberry, who does not at first remember his life in London, but is finally coaxed to remember his life with the Cabby, although his perspective is quite different. Strawberry is persuaded to allow Digory to ride on his back in order to reach Aslan faster and present his petition to him. Meanwhile, the other animals have discovered Uncle Andrew, who is not able to understand the language of the speaking animals. When he sees Digory and Polly leaving with the other animals, he believes they will be eaten along with the magic rings, leaving him with no way back to his own world. When the remaining animals approach him, he becomes frightened and faints, leading them to a debate over whether he is a tree or an animal. They finally conclude he is a tree, plant him in the ground and the elephant douses him with water.

When Strawberry catches up with Aslan and his councilors, Digory slips to the ground and falls down before Aslan, presenting his request for help to him. Digory is expecting the Lion to give him either a yes or no answer, but instead he turns to the animals and announces that "This is the Boy who did it." At first Digory wonders what he has done. Aslan announces that there is an evil witch loose in Narnia, and asks Digory to explain how she came to be here. Dropping his head in shame, Digory explains that he is the one who brought her to this place. Aslan asks why he brought her here. He answers that he was trying to get her out of his world and return her to her own world. Aslan then asks Digory how she came to be in his world. Digory first blames it on his uncle, telling Aslan how Andrew sent Polly to the other world and he had to go and rescue her. In his narrative, Digory says he and Polly met the witch and she just held on to them. At this point, Aslan interrupts him with a questioning voice, saying, "you *met* the witch?" Digory is now forced to admit he woke her up. He must take responsibility for his actions, admitting that Polly did not want to ring the bell and wake her up, but he insisted. At first, he says he was enchanted and could not help himself, but Aslan again forces him to take responsibility for his actions, admitting he was not enchanted, but that he merely wanted to ring the bell and see what would happen. Digory's hopes now sink. He does not think there is any chance he will be able to get help for his mother now. Aslan now turns his attention to the others present, announcing that evil has indeed entered this world before it is even seven hours old. As all eyes look at him, Digory wishes the ground could open up and swallow him. Aslan tells them further that the worst of the evil will fall on him, but it is a long way off. He also prophesies that, just as Adam's race has brought the evil in, Adam's race will be instrumental in defeating the evil. Aslan signals for Polly and the Cabby to come forward. Aslan tells the Cabby he has known him a long time, and asks if he recognizes him. The Cabby responds he does not know him in the ordinary way of speaking, but the more they speak, the more he feels they have met before. Aslan asks the Cabby if he would like to live in this land forever. He responds that he is a married man, and his wife is still in London. However, if she could see this land, he is sure she would want to be here, too. At this, Aslan opens his mouth widely and sends out a long, single note which is so powerful Polly is sure anyone hearing it would have to obey it. Suddenly a young woman appears beside her, apparently interrupted in the middle of doing her laundry. She curtsies to Aslan, and goes to stand beside the Cabby. Aslan announces they are to be the first King and Queen of Narnia. The Cabby protests on the grounds that they do not have the education for such a position. Aslan asks him several questions, mainly whether he would rule all of the people and creatures fairly and remember they are not slaves but free subjects. He also asks if the Cabby will defend the land against all invaders, leading his army and being the last to retreat. He replies he has never been in battle, but will try his best. Aslan tells him that is all that can be expected of a King. The Cabby and his wife are to be the first King and Queen of Narnia, and their children and grandchildren will rule in Narnia and Archenland, which is over the southern mountains. Aslan then turns to Polly, asking if she has forgiven Digory for his abuse of her when they were in Charn. She replies that she has. They have made up.

SUGGESTED ACTIVITIES CHAPTERS 10-11

1. Since these chapters describe the animals as they first emerge in Narnia, this might be a good time to visit the zoo and observe the different animals mentioned.

2. In this chapter, Digory is required to take responsibility for his actions, rather than blaming someone else or the circumstances (I was under an enchantment) for what happened. Ask students to write an essay about a time in their life when they tried to blame something they did on someone else or on the circumstances that were happening. What happened to cause them to have to take responsibility for their actions?

3. Ask students to choose one of the scenes from this sections and illustrated it: the animals emerging from the ground; the animals debating over what Uncle Andrew is; Uncle Andrew being planted in the ground; Digory riding on Strawberry as they try to catch up to Aslan; Digory before Aslan as he is forced to admit his guilt; the Cabby and his wife being announced as King and Queen.

VOCABULARY CHAPTERS 10-11

Satyrs:	(n)	a woodland creature depicted as having the pointed ears, legs, and short horns of a goat and a fondness for unrestrained revelry
Naiad:	(n)	*Greek Mythology* one of the nymphs who lived in and presided over brooks, springs, and fountains
cherish:	(v)	to hold dear; treat with care and affection
perky:	(adj)	lively; cheerful
jackdaw:	(n)	a black and gray Old World crowlike bird
repress:	(v)	curb; restrain
witless:	(adj)	lacking wit or understanding; foolish
justice:	(n)	fairness
plucked:	(v)	to pull something from
council:	(n)	an official body of lawmakers
thicket:	(n)	a dense growth of bushes or small trees
sarcastic:	(adj)	a cutting or contemptuous remark
bowler:	(adj)	a stiff felt hat with rounded crown and narrow brim
dispute:	(v)	to struggle against or over
foremost:	(adj)	first in time, place, or order
sagacious:	(adj)	of keen mind; shrewd
enchanted:	(adj)	bewitched
cockney:	(n)	a native of London and especially of the East End of London

QUESTIONS CHAPTERS 10-11

1. As a result of what the Lion has said, what happens to the trees?

2. What is the Lion's name? How do the children learn his name? Who speaks up in a voice that is different from the others they are hearing?

3. What is the tone of the scene as Narnia begins? (The tone is the mood or feeling of a literary work)

4. In the midst of the joy of Narnia's beginning, what does Aslan reveal?

5. What does Digory reveal to Polly and the Cabby about his plans?

6. When the creatures see Uncle Andrew, what do they think he is?

7. When the children and the Cabby catch up with Strawberry and the horse begins to remember his former life, how is his perspective different from that of the Cabby?

8. What is Strawberry's response when asked if he will allow Digory to ride on his back to catch up to Aslan?

9. How is Uncle Andrew's perception of what has happened different than that of the others involved?

10. What do the animals finally decide Uncle Andrew is? What do they do with him?

11. When Digory finally asks Aslan to help his mother, what does Aslan cause Digory to do?

12. As Aslan is questioning him, what does Digory try to do at first?

13. Read Gen 3:11-12. How does this compare with Adam's sin before God?

14. Read 2 Chron. 7:14; Prov. 28:13; Jer. 3:13; 1 Jn 1:9; Acts 3:19; What must we do in order to be honest with ourselves before God?

15. Once Digory is able to admit his guilt in the situation, what does he believe this will do to his chances of helping his mother?

16. What is the reaction of the beasts to the news Aslan has given them?

17. What does Aslan tell them?

18. When Aslan speaks to the Cabby, what does he ask him? What does his response suggest?

19. What does Aslan offer to the Cabby? What is his response? What does Aslan do?

20. What announcement does Aslan make concerning the Cabby and his wife?

ANSWERS TO QUESTIONS CHAPTERS 10-11

1. The trees suddenly become alive, producing Fauns and Satyrs and Dwarfs.

2. The Lion's name is Aslan. The children learn his name as all of the creatures emerging from the woods surround him and bow down to him, declaring, "Hail, Aslan." The voice that speaks up that is different from the others is Strawberry, the horse.

3. The tone is light and merry, full of happiness, joy and laughter.

4. He tells them, that even though Narnia is only a few hours old, there is already an evil which has entered this new world.

5. He tells them he wants to go to Aslan and appeal to him for help for his mother.

6. They think Uncle Andrew must be the "Neevil" Aslan has spoken of.

7. Strawberry remembers being the one who had to pull the carriage while the Cabby sat up on the seat behind him; he remembers doing all of the work while the Cabby was sitting. Strawberry remembers the land being hard and cruel, with no grass and only hard stones. The Cabby, on the other hand, believes he has always done his best to care for Strawberry with love and concern, giving him oats when he could afford it, rubbing him with a warm cloth when it was cold and rubbing him down after they have been out working.

8. He agrees to allow Digory to ride on his back, but asks if he has a lump of sugar like he remembers from the other world.

9. Uncle Andrew has not heard the animals talking, and did not recognize Aslan's song as a song. He has only heard them all making animal noises – including Aslan. He is terribly frightened by the entire episode, and does not realize at all that he can communicate with the animals or that they can communicate with him.

10. They finally decide he must be a tree, and "plant" him in the ground, covering his legs up to the tops of his boots in mud. The elephant then sprays him with water to make sure his is well watered.

11. Aslan causes Digory to admit it was he who was responsible for bringing the Witch into Narnia in the first place.

12. At first he tries to place the blame on the magic and Uncle Andrew, then he tries to blame his natural human curiosity – he couldn't help himself.

13. Adam tried to blame Eve for his sin, and even blamed God for giving her to him – "It is the woman **you** gave me" that caused me to eat.

14. We have to come to terms with our own guilt – admit our own responsibility for our actions, and not blame anyone else.

15. He believes his actions have destroyed all possibility of his getting help for his mother from Aslan.

16. They all look at Digory, causing him to wish the ground will open up and swallow him.

17. Aslan tells them that, although there will be a price to pay for the evil that has come into the world, he will bear the worst of the cost, and because Adam's race has brought the evil into Narnia, Adam's race will play a part in bringing an end to the evil.

18. He asks the Cabby if he recognizes him. The cabby says he does not recognize him in that form, but he believes he may have known him in another form, which suggests the Cabby was a worshiper of Christ in this world.

19. Aslan offers to let the Cabby live in the land of Narnia forever. He replies that he has a wife in the other world, and they are only common people. Aslan brings his wife into Narnia.

20. The Cabby and his wife are to be the first King and Queen of Narnia, and their children and grandchildren are to reign over Narnia and Archenland, which lies to the south of Narnia.

CHAPTERS 12-13

Digory is standing uncomfortably, concerned that he may start to cry or say something ridiculous. Aslan turns to him, asking if he is ready to undo the wrong he has done to the sweet country of Narnia on the day of its birth. Digory begins to protest, failing to understand how he can do anything to make things right, since the witch has run away. Aslan stops his protests, firmly repeating his question. Digory replies that he is ready. It has occurred to him to strike a deal with Aslan; helping him in exchange for Aslan's help with his mother. However, he realizes that Aslan is not the kind with whom one can make bargains. Feeling his hopes dying away, Digory looks for the first time into the face of the Lion, pleading with tears for help for his mother. He is surprised to see corresponding tears in Aslan's eyes. Aslan explains that he understands Digory's great grief – he alone in Narnia can. His desire at this point, though, is to bring some protection to Narnia before the Witch returns, which she will. He needs Digory to bring him the seed from which a tree will grow which will keep her out of the land for some time to come. Digory agrees to do it, not knowing how, but believing he will be able to do it. Aslan bows down and gives him a kiss, empowering Digory with a new strength and courage. Aslan directs Digory's attention to the West, where there is a mountain range with a waterfall. He explains that Narnia ends where the waterfall comes down, and Digory must journey through the mountains until he finds a green valley with a blue lake, wlled around by mountains of ice. At the end of the lake there is a steep green hill with a garden on its peak. In the center of the garden is a tree, and Digory is to pick an apple from that tree and bring it back to Aslan. Digory wonders how he can possibly manage, but does not want to seem to be making excuses. He tells Aslan that he hopes he is not in any hurry, but Aslan informs him he will have help on his journey. Aslan now turns to Strawberry, and inquires if he would like to be a winged horse. Trying not to be too eager, he only responds, "If you wish, Aslan," but it is obvious he is thrilled at the idea. Aslan immediately transforms him into a winged horse, changing his name to Fledge. Aslan asks if Fledge will be willing to carry Digory to the mountain valley on his back, and he replies that he would be happy to. He remembers carrying things like that on his back long ago when there were green fields and sugar. Aslan takes note that the Cabby's wife, who is now Queen Helen, is conferring with Polly, and asks what they are discussing. Queen Helen informs him that Polly would like to accompany Digory, if Aslan would approve. He defers to Fledge, who agrees as long as the elephant does not want to go as well. Aslan instructs Fledge not to fly too high, and to avoid the tops of the great ice mountains. He should look for the green places and fly through them. As they approach the waterfall, Fledge tells them he will have to do some zig-zagging, and warns them to hold on tight. As they look back over the land of Narnia below them, Digory expresses a desire for someone to explain to them something about what all those places are, and Polly responds that they are not anywhere yet; the world only began today. Digory says that one day people will get there, and the places will have histories. Polly expresses relief that there is no history now, because that means no one will be made to learn battles and dates and such. After they have succeeded in flying over the tops of the cliffs, the sun seems to fill the sky, but not warm them. Fledge is also tiring, and suggests they find a place to spend the night. Digory mentions it must be time for supper as well. Once Fledge has landed and the children have dismounted, he begins to feast on the available grass, but Digory complains again of being hungry. Fledge encourages the children to join him in his feast, but they explain to him that they are not grass eaters. When Digory crossly points out that it seems like someone should have arranged for their meals, Fledge replies that he is sure Aslan would have if they had asked. Polly asks if he wouldn't know they need meals without being asked. Fledge replies he is sure he does, but thinks he prefers to be asked. Digory suggests Polly can use her ring and go home to get some food, but she refuses to leave Digory, and mentions she has the remains of a bag of toffee in her pocket. Digory reminds her she must be careful to put her hand in her pocket without touching the ring. Since there are nine pieces left, Digory suggests they each eat four, then bury the last piece. After all, if the lamp-post could grow into a light tree, maybe the toffee could grow into a toffee tree. When they have all finished eating, Fledge lies down and spreads his wings over each of the children. As the stars come out, they talk about the experience of seeing the new world come into being, and Digory talks of how much he wanted to get something to heal his mother. Instead he has been sent on this mission. They are just beginning to become sleepy when Polly hears something. Digory suggests maybe it was only the wind, but Fledge agrees with Polly. He gets to his feet and they all look. Polly is certain she sees a dark figure gliding away in a westerly direction, but they are not able to find anything for sure. The children settle back in and are quickly asleep; Fledge stays awake much longer, but eventually joins them in sleep.

In the morning, Polly awakens Digory and Fledge to let them know the toffee has grown into a toffee tree, and it is a beautiful morning. Digory decides he wants to bathe in the river before he eats. When he returns, Polly takes her turn, declaring she bathes in the river as well, but since she does not swim, that is not certain. Fledge goes and stands midstream in the water, stooping down to drink, shaking his mane and neighing. The fruit of the toffee tree is not exactly like toffee, but it is delicious, and Digory and Polly enjoy it thoroughly. Soon they mount the horse and the journey begins anew. They are enjoying it much more this time, as the sun is at their backs, and the day is new. A smell comes to them that is warm and golden, seeming to come from all of the most delicious fruits and flowers of the world, and the children ask where it is coming from. Fledge points out the valley with the lake in it, and they all realize this must be The Place. Fledge lands and the children tumble off and begin the steep ascent to the garden. When they reach the garden, they find it walled in with high golden gates facing the east. On the gates there is and inscription, and Fledge and Polly realize that only Digory will be able to go in. The inscription states that those who steal or climb the wall will find their heart's desire or despair. Only those who are taking the fruit for others will be allowed. Digory realizes he cannot eat the fruit for himself, but must only take the fruit to Aslan. Wondering how to open the gates, he places his hand on it, and it immediately swings inward. Digory realizes at once that this is a very private and solemn place. Instinctively knowing that the tree in the middle of the garden is the correct one, he crosses to it and picks one of the apples. However, he is tempted to look at it and smell it before putting it in his pocket. Immediately he feels an insatiable hunger and thirst and longing for the fruit. He considers taking a second apple for himself, and is mulling over the possibilities of partial disobedience when he looks up and spies a beautiful bird roosting above his head. The bird is eyeing him through a tiny slit in its eye. He makes his way to the gate and turns for one look back at the garden. He is shocked to discover he is not alone, but is in the presence of the Witch, who has just consumed an apple and is discarding the core. The juice is darker than expected and has left a terrible stain around her mouth. Digory guesses she has climbed over the wall, and is experiencing the consequences of the last line of the inscription; that of getting one's heart's desire and despair with it. She looks stronger, prouder and triumphant, and yet is a deathly white. Digory runs as fast as he can to Fledge, urging Polly to jump on to they can escape. However, the Witch has climbed the wall again, and is right behind him, talking to him in a sweet voice and trying to dissuade him from leaving. Her first tactic is to attempt to convince him he should eat the apple and it will allow him to live forever, ruling with her either in this world or his. He replies he would not want to outlive everyone he knows. She quickly changes her tune, speaking of his ailing mother and how she could be healed by this apple. He can use his ring to take himself back to his own world in order to save his mother. When he states that he has promised Aslan he will bring the fruit to him, and he must keep his promise, she accuses him of being cruel and unfeeling. For a minute he is torn, the desire to help his mother causing him to hesitate until the Witch makes the fatal mistake of suggesting he leave Polly behind and no one in his world would know anything about the whole story of what has happened here. Of course, she does not know that Polly has her own ring, but her statement has revealed her true nature. Digory asks her when she became so fond of his mother, and Polly urges him to get away now. He orders Fledge up, and they are back in Narnia by nightfall. He walks up to Aslan and presents to him the apple.

SUGGESTED ACTIVITIES CHAPTERS 12-13

1. Have students make posters or otherwise illustrate the garden to which Digory has been sent.

2. There are parallels between this story and the story of the Garden of Eden. Assign a compare/contrast between this story and the story of the temptation of Adam and Eve in the Garden of Eden in Genesis.

3. If it is the right time of year, have students plant a garden at the home of a senior citizen, or bring some potted flowers to a nursing home to cheer up someone who has little contact with young people. Have them prepare a presentation about the garden, or about the "toffee tree" planted by Digory and Polly.

VOCABULARY CHAPTERS 12-13

blub	(v)	cry
despair	(n)	utter loss of hope
shied	(v)	to start suddenly aside through fright
curvetted	(v)	a prancing leap of a horse
cataracts	(n)	steep rapids in a river
turf	(n)	the upper layer of soil bound by grass and roots into a close mat
solemnly	(adv)	highly serious
saffron	(n)	a deep orange powder from the flower of a crocus used to color and flavor foods
pelt	(v)	to hurry
vaulted	(v)	to leap vigorously especially by aid of the hands or a pole
simpleton	(n)	fool
fatal	(adj)	causing ruin
cantering	(v)	a horse's 3-beat gait resembling but smoother and slower than a gallop
nymphs	(n)	any of the lesser goddesses in ancient mythology represented as maidens living in the mountains, forests, meadows, and waters

The Magician's Nephew

QUESTIONS CHAPTERS 12-13

1. What is the question Aslan asks Digory?

2. What is his first response? What does Aslan's repetition of the question indicate?

3. What does Digory realize when he looks into Aslan's eyes for the first time?

4. What is Aslan planning to do?

5. What is Digory's mission?

6. When Digory sees the full extent of what he must do, what does he think?

7. How does Aslan provide a way for him to overcome the difficulty of the obstacles he faces?

8. According to the Cabby's wife, who wants to accompany Digory on his quest?

9. What is Fledge's response?

10. When they stop for the night, what do they discover about their provisions?

11. When Digory complains that it seems Aslan should have arranged for their meals, what does Fledge tell him? What does Fledge tell Polly about Aslan's nature? How is this similar to the nature of God?

12. How do the children solve the problem of what to eat? What do they decide to do in order to provide for the next day?

13. What happens as they settle down to sleep?

14. What do they discover in the morning?

15. When they reach the garden, what misconception do Fledge and Polly discover they have had about the mission?

16. What are the two rules given in the inscription on the gates, and what are the consequences spoken of for those who break the rules?

17. Why do the gates open for Digory?

18. When Digory picks the fruit, what does he do that he should not have done?

19. How is this temptation like the temptation to ring the golden bell in Charn? How is it different? Why do you think Digory was sent on this mission, and why was it important for him to face this temptation?

20. Just as Digory overcomes the temptation to eat the apple, whom does he discover? How did she get there? What has she been doing? What does Digory realize about the last line of the inscription?

21. What does she try to convince Digory the apple will do for him if he eats it? Compare this to the strategy used by the serpent with Eve in the Garden of Eden in Gen. 3.

22. When that tactic does not work, what does she try to do to convince Digory not to take the apple back to Aslan?

23. Why is it important to the Witch to keep the apple from Aslan?

24. Although Digory feels more temptation on this point because of his love for his mother, what happens that allows him to see through the Witch and understand her real nature?

25. When Digory has doubts about whether he is doing the right thing in taking the apple to Aslan rather than taking it to his mother, what thought convinces him that this is right?

The Magician's Nephew

ANSWERS TO QUESTIONS CHAPTERS 12-13

1. "Are you ready to undo the wrong you have done to my sweet country of Narnia on the very day of its birth?"

2. At first he begins to make excuses, saying he doesn't see what he can do; the Queen has run away. He is not able to finish before Aslan interrupts him, repeating the question. He wants Digory to know that he will not allow him to escape taking responsibility for what he has done. He must face up to his guilt, and do what must be done to make things right.

3. Aslan has tears in his eyes. He has as much compassion for Digory's mother as Digory does.

4. He is planning to plant a tree that will prevent the Witch from entering Narnia for a long period of time so that the land will have time to grow and prosper before she returns.

5. He must go to a mountain that is outside of the boundaries of Narnia, where he will find a garden. He must go to that garden, pick an apple and bring it back to Aslan, so that he can plant the seeds. The seeds from this apple will produce the tree which will protect Narnia.

6. He thinks the task is bigger than he can handle, but has decided that it is useless to make excuses to Aslan. Instead he simply tells him he won't be able to get there and back very quickly.

7. He turns Strawberry into a flying horse, changing his name to Fledge and asking him if he will be willing to carry Digory on his journey.

8. Polly

9. Fledge is willing to take another person, but jokes that he hopes the Elephant doesn't want to come as well.

10. Although there is grass for Fledge to eat, the children have no food.

11. He tells Digory that he is sure Aslan would have provided food for them if they had asked. When Polly asks if Aslan doesn't know they need food without their asking, Fledge responds that he thinks Aslan likes to be asked. God knows what we need before we ask Him, but He prefers for us to go to Him in prayer and present our petitions to Him.

12. Polly discovers she has a part of a bag of toffee in her pocket. There are nine of them, so they decide to eat four each, and plant one of them, believing that if the lamp-post grew in this land, then the toffee might also grow into a toffee tree.

13. Polly hears a sound and believes she sees a shadow moving in the woods, and Fledge has the same feeling.

14. The toffee has grown into a tree with fruit that is like an apple, but has a taste that is similar to toffee.

15. They have believed all along that they will be able to accompany Digory into the garden, but they know immediately that his mission is personal and private, and he must accomplish it alone.

16. The rules state that (1) a person must enter through the gates or not at all; and (2) the fruit must be taken for others or left alone. The consequences for those who climb over the wall or steal the fruit are that they will find their heart's desire and find despair.

17. The gates open for Digory because he has been sent on the mission by Aslan. He is following the rules inscribed on the gates – entering through the gates and seeking the fruit for another rather than himself.

18. When he picks the fruit, instead of immediately placing it into his pocket, he looks at it and smells it, which causes him to desire the fruit for himself.

19. Just like the bell at Charn, Digory is drawn to the fruit through the magical spell that is on the object. He feels the strength of the temptation to eat the apple just as he felt the temptation to ring the bell. However, in Charn he impulsively gave in to the temptation without giving thought to the consequences of his actions. This time he used greater restraint and used his past failure to help him in resisting the urge to eat. It was important for Digory to face this temptation in order to prove, both to himself and to Aslan that he was willing to learn from his previous disobedience and allow himself to be disciplined by a desire to obey Aslan rather than his own desires. Aslan knew the outcome, but Digory's commitment to obedience had to be tested for Digory's sake, much as Abraham's willingness to sacrifice Isaac had to be tested for Abraham's sake.

20. He finds that Jadis is in the garden with him. It is obvious she has entered by climbing over the wall. She has just finished eating one of the apples. When he looks at her, he immediately sees a visual image of the last line of the inscription. Jadis looks stronger, prouder and more triumphant than ever, but she also is deadly white.

21. She tries to convince Digory that the apple will allow him to live forever. This is exactly the strategy employed by the serpent in the Garden of Eden. (Gen. 3:4 : "You will not surely die, the serpent said to the woman.")

22. She tries to convince him he should take the apple to his mother, rather than taking it to Aslan.

23. She does not want Digory to return the apple to Aslan because his plan is to plant a tree that will keep her out of Narnia for a period of time. In addition, she knows that for Digory to complete his mission is to demonstrate his obedience to Aslan, strengthening his position and weakening hers.

24. She suggests Digory leave Polly behind and return to his own world to save his mother, so that no one there will know of this world. Digory knows Polly has her own ring and can return on her own if she wants, but the Witch's suggestion reveals her selfishness. Digory's eyes are immediately opened to the fact that her only concern is for herself and what she wants, not his mother.

25. He remembers the tears that were in Aslan's eyes as he thought of Digory's mother with compassion.

CHAPTERS 14-15

Aslan praises Digory on a job well done when Digory delivers the apple to him, and Digory realizes this story will be repeated in Narnia for generations to come. No longer ashamed, Digory is able to look Aslan directly in the eyes. Aslan informs Digory that no one else is qualified to sow the seed of the tree that is to protect Narnia, and Digory does as he is told. Aslan next turns his attention to the coronation of the King and Queen of Narnia, Frank and Helen. Both the children and Fledge are amazed at the transformation of the two. They have truly become royal. Aslan commands the animals to untangle some trees to see what can be found there. It turns out that the animals have placed Uncle Andrew in something of a cage, using the trees to pen him in. Different animals have thrown in their various favorite foods, some of which are inedible to Andrew, and he is in a mess. The final offering is a nest of bees thrown in to him by the bear, covering Andrew with sticky honey. The animals are calling him "Brandy" because that is the only sound coming out of his mouth as he calls for his favorite liquor. He is in such a sate when he is removed from the trees that Polly appeals to Aslan to calm the old man and then do something to prevent him from returning to Narnia. Aslan asks her if she really thinks he would want to return, and when she begins to explain some of his ideas, he responds that he is full of folly. The effects they have seen are not lasting, and have come about only as a result of Aslan's song. Furthermore, Andrew has cut himself off from the ability to hear Aslan. He will not be able to comfort him, but instead causes him to fall into a deep sleep. Turning his attention back to the coronation, Aslan commands the dwarves to craft crowns from the golden and silver trees that have grown from the coins that fell from Uncle Andrew's pockets. Immediately after the King and Queen have been crowned, Aslan directs their attention to the tree which has grown from the apple. He tells them the tree will be their shield to protect them from the Witch for hundreds of years, because she will not come near Narnia as long as it is there. She will not be able to tolerate the smell of the fruit. Digory and Polly explain that she has already eaten one of the apples, and Aslan lets them know that this is exactly why she will find the fruit to be a horror to her. Although she has gained eternal youth, she will live in eternal misery because of her wickedness. Aslan brings up Digory's temptation, and clarifies to him what would have happened if he had taken the stolen fruit to his mother, stating it would have been better for her to have died. However, he now invites Digory to take one of the apples to his mother, stating that because it is not stolen, it will bring eternal joy. Digory is beside himself, and picks one of the apples to the cheers of all the others. Forgetting to thank Aslan, he turns and asks if they can go home now.

Aslan lets them know that they will not need the rings when they are with him, and takes them to Wood Between the Worlds, where Uncle Andrew is still asleep. Before sending them home, Aslan explains that he has a warning and a command to give them. He shows them the pool into which they first jumped, which led them to Charn. The pool has dried up, and Aslan makes it clear that the demise of the world of Charn has led to the end of this pool. He warns them that their world is moving in the same direction as Charn, and they should beware. Next he commands them to take the magic rings from Uncle Andrew and bury them so that no one will be able to use them again. They find themselves back in London, in the middle of the same fracas that was going on when they left. They realize that no time has passed in this world. As the crowd is searching for Jadis, the children and Andrew are able to escape into the house. The people have not noticed the children at all, and Andrew is in such a mess that they do not even recognize him. The housemaid opens the door and lets him in, enjoying the entire show immensely. Uncle Andrew goes immediately to his attic laboratory, and the children fear they will have difficulty securing the rings from him, but discover quickly he is only after his brandy. When he takes the bottle to his bedroom, Digory dispatches Polly to get the rings while he takes the apple to his mother. After eating the apple, Digory's mother falls into a peaceful, non-drug induced sleep. When the doctor comes the next day, he believes Mrs. Kirke is showing improvement, but does not want to raise false hopes in Digory. Digory buries the core of the apple in the backyard, and when Polly brings the rings over the next day, they bury them in a circle around the core. They find the tree has already begun to grow, even though it is not as miraculous a growth as in Narnia. While Digory's mother is recovering her health, his father sends word from India that his Great Uncle Kirke has died, so Digory's father will be coming home to retire to the large family home in the country. Uncle Andrew comes to live with the family, but never practices magic again. Digory and Polly remain friends for life. Digory becomes a professor, and when a storm blows the tree down, he cannot bring himself to have it cut up into firewood. He has it made into a wardrobe which is brought to the country home. Of course, he discovers it still has some of the Narnian magic in it when another child enters Narnia through that wardrobe. In Narnia, the place where the lamp-post grew becomes known as Lantern Waste, and the light burns day and night until hundreds of years later when it is discovered by another child who enters Narnia from our world.

SUGGESTED ACTIVITIES CHAPTERS 14-15

1. Ask students to choose their favorite scene in the book, write a skit and act it out.

2. Assign a compare/contrast in which students compare and contrast Digory and Polly at the beginning of the story and at the end. In what ways are they the same? How have they changed?

3. Ask students to look at the warning given to the children. Obviously, it is particularly pointing to the tyrants coming into power during World War II. However, there are still tyrants in this world. Have students write an essay, or have a discussion as if they are receiving this warning from Aslan, and tell what they can do in their lifetime to change the way things are in this world.

VOCABULARY CHAPTERS 14-15

conceited	(adj)	excessively high opinion of one's self or ability
coronation	(n)	the act or ceremony of crowning a monarch
cunning	(adj)	wiliness and trickery
coop	(n)	a small enclosure or building usually for poultry
bombarded	(v)	to attack with bombs, shells, or missiles
volleys	(n)	a burst of many things at once
lobbed	(v)	to throw, hit, or propel something in a high arc
folly	(n)	foolishness
loathe	(v)	o dislike greatly
tyrants	(n)	a ruler who governs oppressively or brutally
wan	(adj)	sickly; feeble; weak
counterpane	(n)	bedspread
trowel	(n)	a small flat or scooplike implement used in gardening
fortnight	(n)	two weeks

Novel Insights Plus

QUESTIONS CHAPTERS 14-15

1. When Digory brings the apple to Aslan, what honor is given to him?

2. When the children turn their attention to the new King and Queen, in what ways are they different?

3. What have the animals done to Uncle Andrew?

4. What is Polly's request to Aslan for him? What is Aslan's response?

5. What does Aslan say about Uncle Andrew's plans for Narnia?

6. What does Aslan do to Uncle Andrew?

7. From where does the gold and silver for the crowns come?

8. When Aslan shows them the tree that has grown, what do Polly and Digory tell him about the Witch?

9. How have her actions affected her?

10. What confession does Digory make? What else does Aslan lead him to confess?

11. What does Aslan tell would have happened if he had given in to his temptation?

12. What lesson does this teach us?

13. As he prepares to send them to their own world, what is the warning Aslan gives to Polly and Digory?

14. What is the command he gives them?

15. When they return, what do they discover?

16. What happens to Digory's mother when she eats the apple?

17. What happens to the tree that grows from the apple seeds?

18. What happens in Narnia?

19. What is the name of the place where the lamp-post has grown?

20. What happens to Uncle Andrew?

ANSWERS TO QUESTIONS CHAPTERS 14-15

1. He is allowed to plant the seeds that are to grow the tree to protect Narnia from the Witch.

2. Although both have more a more noble appearance, the Cabby, who is now Frank, has changed dramatically. He has an air of courage and kindness that he did not have when he was in London, and he has lost the shrewdness and cunning he seemed to have in London.

3. They have enclosed him in a cage of trees, holding him captive until they can appeal to Aslan for help in dealing with him. Different species of animals have tried to feed him with various forms of food, leaving Andrew in a mess. They have named him "Brandy" as a result of his crying out for brandy to drink, and want to keep him as a pet.

4. Polly asks Aslan to do something to calm Uncle Andrew down. He tells her he will not be able to do anything for him, because Uncle Andrew has closed his ears to the ability to hear Aslan speak. If Aslan tries to speak to him, he will only hear growling and snarling.

5. He tells Polly Uncle Andrew's plans were foolish.

6. He causes him to fall asleep.

7. Trees have grown from the gold and silver coins that fell from Uncle Andrew's pockets when the animals tried to "plant" him upside down.

8. They tell Aslan that Jadis has already eaten the fruit.

9. Aslan tells the children that, although she will have the ability to have eternal youth, she will also live with eternal misery caused by the wicked condition of her heart.

10. He confesses that he was tempted to eat the apple himself. Aslen then leads him to confess that Jadis tempted him to take the apple home to his mother without bringing it to Aslan as he had been instructed.

11. Although the apple would have healed his mother, the fact that it was gained through disobedience would lead to misery for his mother, to the extent that it would be better for her to die.

12. Obedience is always better than disobedience, even when it may seem like following the course of disobedience will lead to what you want more than anything else. Anything gained through disobedience will lead to unhappiness in the end.

13. He takes them to the pool that had led them to Charn, and shows them how it has dried up because that world has died through all of its wickedness. He warns them that their world is moving in that direction, and they need to be on their guard to keep it from going that way.

14. He commands them to take all of the magic rings from Uncle Andrew and bury them so that no one will be able to use them again.

15. No time has passed in their world. The scene outside Digory's house is exactly as it was when they disappeared from the street and into the Wood Between the Worlds.

16. She immediately falls into a peaceful sleep, and by the next day is showing improvement. Soon she is fully recovered and is able to enjoy playing with Digory and Polly.

17. Eventually it is blown over by a storm when Digory is an adult, and he has the wood made into a wardrobe.

18. In Narnia, everyone lives in peace and harmony for many hundred years. King Frank and Queen Helen and their children are very happy, and their children marry the nymphs and the wood-gods and river-gods. Their second son becomes the King of Archenland. The lamp-post which was planted by the Witch glows day and night until it is discovered by another child from our world (Lucy Pevensie).

19. Lantern Waste

20. When Digory's father returns from India and the family moves to the large family home in the country, Uncle Andrew comes to live with them, never desiring to practice magic again.

VOCABULARY TEST CHAPTER 1
THE MAGICIAN'S NEPHEW

I. Matching: Place the letter of the correct answer in the blank: Choose the word that is the closest synonym to the vocabulary word:

1. ____vain   A. pirates
2. ____beastly   B. simpleton
3. ____indignantly   C. flee
4. ____mad   D. futile
5. ____fishy   E. shrewd
6. ____coiner   F. disagreeable
7. ____cistern   G. disheveled
8. ____smugglers   H. insane
9. ____draughty   I. tank
10. _____bunk   J. resentfully
11. _____tousled   K. questionable
12. _____cunning   L. breezy
13. _____duffer   M. inventor

Novel Insights Plus

ANSWERS TO VOCABULARY TEST CHAPTER 1

THE MAGICIAN'S NEPHEW

I. Matching:

1. D
2. F
3. J
4. H
5. K
6. M
7. I
8. A
9. L
10. C
11. G
12. E
13. B

VOCABULARY TEST CHAPTERS 2-3
THE MAGICIAN'S NEPHEW

I.   Multiple Choice: Circle the letter of the correct answer:

1. The word that means a cleaning woman is:
   a. chary
   b. lackey
   c. charwoman
   d. spinster

2. The spirit or character of the ideal knight is:
   a. madrigal
   b. chivalry
   c. beatific
   d. maxim

3. Those who are distinguished for their wisdom are called:
   a. anathema
   b. coquettes
   c. arpeggios
   d. sages

4. Something that is of a superior nature is:
   a. ancillary
   b. covert
   c. noble
   d. aberration

5. Something that differs from the usual or is peculiar is:
   a. perfunctory
   b. queer
   c. splenetic
   d. idyllic

6. When Uncle Andrew described himself as an **expert** magician, the word he used was:
   a. adept
   b. adjure
   c. abeyance
   d. appellation

7. Something that is not clear or distinct is:
   a. venal
   b. votary
   c. veracious
   d. vague

8. The slang word Digory uses for talking too much is:
   a. querulous
   b. babbling
   c. gassing
   d. jawing

9. An institution for the care of the needy, sick or especially the insane is called a:
   a. apothecary
   b. asylum
   c. apiary
   d. amulet

10. When Uncle Andrew said that the predetermined course of his life was high and lonely, he used the word:
    a. destiny
    b. future
    c. fate
    d. doom

11. Something that shows intellectual depth or insight is:
    a. pragmatic
    b. pernicious
    c. profound
    d. propaganda

12. Something dignified or solemn could be described as:
    a. gentry
    b. grave
    c. grandiose
    d. gossamer

13. Another word for something that is absurd is:
    a. perspicuous
    b. precedent
    c. peccadillo
    d. preposterous

ANSWERS TO VOCABULARY TEST CHAPTERS 2-3
THE MAGICIAN'S NEPHEW

I. Multiple Choice:

1. c
2. b
3. d
4. c
5. b
6. a
7. d
8. c
9. b
10. a
11. c
12. b
13. d

VOCABULARY TEST CHAPTERS 4-6

THE MAGICIAN'S NEPHEW

I. **Fill in the Blank: Use the words from the Word Bank at the end of this section to fill in the blanks:**

1. Polly said, "I've had enough of this place, and I've had enough of you, you beastly, stuck-up, _____ pig.
2. The Witch told Uncle Andrew to go and _____ for her a chariot, or flying carpet, or whatever people here used for transportation.
3. As the children looked at the figures in the great hall, they became crueler and more grim as they went along, until toward the end they were even _____ faces.
4. As she sends Uncle Andrew on his mission, she warns him not to even dream of _____.
5. Uncle Andrew tells the Witch she has put him in a _____ awkward position.
6. When Digory asks Polly to come back and explains he is worried about what will happen if the Witch wanders into his mother's room, Polly agrees that they can forget their disagreement, and call it _____ for the sake of his mother.
7. Uncle Andrew went downstairs and sent a housemaid to get a _____ for the Witch.
8. Digory whispered, "I'll bet this whole room is just stiff with _____. I could feel the magic the moment we came in."
9. When they first arrived, Digory announced that the weather was very funny in this world. He wondered if they had arrived just in time for a thunderstorm or an _____.
10. Digory warned Polly they needed to be very quiet, or their noise might cause something like an _____ in the Alps.

Word Bank:

deucedly	hansom	eclipse	obstinate
pax	avalanche	treachery	procure
enchantments	despairing		

II.   Matching: Place the letter of the correct answer in the blank:

1. ____ pillared   A. a servile follower; underling

2. ____ rubble   B. an outer garment worn especially by men

3. ____ sulky   C. broken fragments especially of a destroyed building

4. ____ bosh   D. familiar

5. ____ minion   E. foolish talk; nonsense

6. ____ shamming   F. having strong upright supports

7. ____ homely   G. morose; moody

8. ____ frockcoat   H. pretending

ANSWERS TO VOCABULARY TEST CHAPTERS 4-6
THE MAGICIAN'S NEPHEW

I. Fill in the Blank:

1. obstinate
2. procure
3. despairing
4. treachery
5. deucedly
6. pax
7. hansom
8. enchantments
9. eclipse
10. avalanche

II. Matching:

1. F
2. C
3. G
4. E
5. A
6. H
7. D
8. B

The Magician's Nephew

VOCABULARY TEST CHAPTERS 7-9

THE MAGICIAN'S NEPHEW

I. **Matching: Place the letter of the correct answer in the blank:**

1. ___ hussy   A. choke; strangle

2. ___ sal volatile   B. pretentious or excessive display

3. ___ lunatic   C. institution for chronic disease or medical supervision

4. ___ rampaging   D. rude; insolent

5. ___ throttle   E. solution used in smelling salts

6. ___ flogging   F. polite acts or expressions

7. ___ impertinent   G. rushing about wildly

8. ___ abominably   H. beating with a rod or whip

9. ___ civilities   I. strap of iron between the shaft & harness on a drawn wagon

10. ___ ostentatious   J. a lewd or brazen woman

11. ___ strab   K. odious; detestable; loathsome

12. ___ sanitorium   L. insane person

ANSWERS TO VOCABULARY TEST CHAPTERS 7-9
THE MAGICIAN'S NEPHEW

I. Matching:

1. J
2. E
3. L
4. G
5. A
6. H
7. D
8. K
9. F
10. B
11. I
12. C

The Magician's Nephew

VOCABULARY TEST CHAPTERS 10-11

THE MAGICIAN'S NEPHEW

I.   Multiple Choice: Circle the letter of the correct answer:

1. When the animals first started to laugh, they tried to **repress** it:
   a. encourage
   b. flatter
   c. insult
   d. restrain

2. Uncle Andrew had been shrinking further and further into the **thicket**:
   a. bare ground
   b. desert cactus
   c. dense bushes or trees
   d. a small fish pond

3. The **sagacious** elephant continued pouring water over Uncle Andrew until it looked like he had taken a bath with his clothes on:
   a. of keen mind; shrewd
   b. cheerful
   c. foolish
   d. slow

4. Out of the river rose the river god with his **Naiad** daughters:
   a. ballet dancers
   b. light-skinned
   c. formula of magic words
   d. water nymphs

5. Aslan told the animals that he would call some of them to his **council**:
   a. list of persons eligible to vote
   b. official body of lawmakers
   c. group of followers
   d. head of the senate

6. There was some **dispute** as to which way Uncle Andrew ought to be put into the hole:
   a. lack of interest
   b. confusion
   c. fear
   d. struggle against or over

7. Aslan told the animals they were no longer dumb and **witless**:
   a. strong
   b. foolish
   c. clever
   d. fat

8. Uncle Andrew saw cool-looking leopards and panthers with **sarcastic** faces staring at him and waving their tails:
   a. having authority
   b. an air of sadness
   c. cutting or contemptuous
   d. reckless bravery

9. Aslan tells the Cabby to treat the animals gently and **cherish** them without letting them go back to their ways so they will stop being talking beasts:
   a. treat with care and affection
   b. look down upon
   c. deeply distrust
   d. thoroughly dislike

10. One **jackdaw** added in a loud voice, "No fear:"
    a. species of animal now extinct
    b. object of non-terrestrial origin
    c. object out of its proper historical time
    d. black & gray Old World crow-like bird

II. Matching: Place the letter of the correct answer in the blank:

1. ____Satyrs   A. bewitched

2. ____perky   B. pull something from

3. ____justice   C. native of the East End of London

4. ____plucked   D. woodland creature that is part goat & has a fondness for revelry

5. ____bowler   E. fairness

6. ____foremost   F. stiff felt hat with rounded crown & narrow brim

7. ____enchanted   G. first in time, place or order

8. ____cockney   H. lively; cheerful

ANSWERS TO VOCABULARY CHAPTERS 10-11
THE MAGICIAN'S NEPHEW

I. Multiple Choice:

1. d
2. c
3. a
4. d
5. b
6. d
7. b
8. c
9. a
10. d

II. Matching:

1. D
2. H
3. E
4. B
5. F
6. G
7. A
8. C

VOCABULARY TEST CHAPTERS 12-13
THE MAGICIAN'S NEPHEW

I.   Matching: Place the letter of the correct answer in the blank:

1.____blub   A. hurry

2.____despair   B. steep rapids in a river

3.____shied   C. causing ruin

4.____curvetted   D. cry

5.____cataracts   E. lesser goddesses living in mountains, forests, meadows & waters

6.____turf   F. start suddenly aside through fright

7.____solemnly   G. horse's 3-beat gait resembling, but smoother & slower than a gallop

8.____saffron   H. upper layer of soil bound by grass & roots into a close mat

9.____pelt   I. fool

10.____vaulted   J. utter loss of hope

11.____simpleton   K. highly serious

12.____fatal   L. prancing leap of a horse

13.____cantering   M. deep orange powder from the flower of a crocus

14.____nymphs   N. leap vigorously with aid of hands or a pole

ANSWERS TO VOCABULARY TEST CHAPTERS 12-13
THE MAGICIAN'S NEPHEW

I. **Matching:**

1. D
2. J
3. F
4. L
5. B
6. H
7. K
8. M
9. A
10. N
11. I
12. C
13. G
14. E

Novel Insights Plus

VOCABULARY TEST CHAPTERS 14-15
THE MAGICIAN'S NEPHEW

I. **Fill in the Blank: Use the words from the Word Bank at the end of this section to fill in the following blanks:**

1. The squirrels _____ Uncle Andrew with _____ of nuts but he only covered his head with his hands and tried to keep out of the way.

2. When Polly told Aslan Uncle Andrew's plans, Aslan said that Uncle Andrew was thinking great _____.

3. Aslan told Digory and Polly that before they were an old man and old woman, their world would be ruled by _____ who do not care for joy or justice or mercy any more than Jadis.

4. Digory and Polly took a _____ and buried all the magic rings.

5. Digory and Polly were present at the _____ of King Frank and Queen Helen.

6. Aslan told Digory that those who steal the fruit find it is good, but they _____ it ever after.

7. About a _____ after eating the apple, Digory's mother was able to sit out in the garden.

8. Digory went into his mother's room with the apple, and saw her propped up with the same _____ pale face that made him want to cry.

9. When Digory presented the fruit to Aslan, and Aslan proclaimed that he had done well, Digory was in no danger of being _____.

10. When he was trying to feed Uncle Andrew, the bear _____ a bee hive over the enclosure and onto Uncle Andrew's head.

11. When he entered his mother's room, Digory saw the colored _____ on her bed and the colored wallpaper, but it all seemed pale in comparison with the apple.

12. When the Cabby became King Frank, all the sharpness and _____ and quarrelsomeness he had picked up in London were gone.

13. The animals had made a sort of _____ around Uncle Andrew to make sure he was safely kept where they had him.

Word Bank:

conceited	coronation	cunning	bombarded	coop
volleys	lobbed	folly	loathe	tyrants
wan	counterpane	trowel	fortnight	

- 88 -

ANSWERS TO VOCABULARY TEST CHAPTERS 14-15
THE MAGICIAN'S NEPHEW

I. Fill in the Blank:

1. bombarded; volleys
2. folly
3. tyrants
4. trowel
5. coronation
6. loathe
7. fortnight
8. wan
9. conceited
10. lobbed
11. counterpane
12. cunning
13. coop

Novel Insights Plus

TEST QUESTIONS
THE MAGICIAN'S NEPHEW

I.   Multiple Choice: Circle the letter of the correct answer:

1. The setting of this story is:
   a. London, England in the 1950s
   b. New York City 1900
   c. London, England, in 1970
   d. London, England at turn of 20th century

2. When Polly first sees Digory next door she thinks it is odd because:
   a. before Digory lived two houses down
   b. his aunt & uncle have no children
   c. he has always stayed in the house
   d. Digory usually plays with the boys

3. When Polly and Digory talk about his Uncle Andrew, it is revealed that most people think Uncle Andrew:
   a. is really smart
   b. has been abducted by aliens
   c. is insane
   d. is an absent minded professor

4. When Digory and Polly accidentally "drop in" to Uncle Andrew's secret laboratory, he has been looking for a child because:
   a. he wants to give them a present
   b. he wants to send one to another world
   c. he wants to adopt one
   d. he wants to play video games with one

5. Uncle Andrew inherited the material necessary to make the magic rings from:
   a. Digory's mother
   b. his great-grandmother
   c. Aslan
   d. his godmother

6. Uncle Andrew discovered the material used to make the rings came from:
   a. the moon
   b. Narnia
   c. Atlantis
   d. Jupiter

7. Digory takes the ring and follows Polly because:
   a. he feels a responsibility to rescue her
   b. Uncle Andrew orders him to
   c. he doesn't want her to have all the fun
   d. he is looking for a way to Narnia

8. When Digory emerges he notices:
   a. he has come out of a pool & is soaking wet
   b. he comes out of a pool & is totally dry
   c. it is very cold
   d. it is very dark

9. Digory and Polly name the place they are in:
   a. Narnia
   b. Charn
   c. Achenland
   d. The Wood Between the Worlds

10. When they arrive at the dying world, a conflict occurs between Polly and Digory over:
    a. whether to live here forever or go home
    b. whether to explore here or go home
    c. whether to tell Andrew about this world
    c. whether or not to go for help

11. When they finally find a room in the castle that has people in it, Polly is entranced with their:
    a. faces
    b. power
    c. clothing
    d. pets

12. Although he knows it is the wrong thing to do, Digory cannot resist the urge to:
    a. ring the bell in the center of the room
    b. throw rocks at the statue-like figures
    c. push the pillars down
    d. make faces at the seated figures

13. As Digory takes his action, Polly notices that:
    a. she wishes he would be more assertive
    b. he is suddenly older
    c. he is being too quiet
    d. he resembles his uncle

14. The consequence of Digory's action is:
    a. they are transported back to earth
    b. nothing happens
    c. the walls fall; the cruelest figure awakens
    d. Aslan suddenly shows up

15. The reaction of the children to the woman standing before them is:
    a. they both think she is wonderful
    b. they are both frightened of her
    c. to Polly she is beautiful; Digory is scared
    d. to Digory she is beautiful; Polly is scared

16. When Jadis hangs onto Digory in order to bring herself into his world, her plans are:
    a. to ask for help to revitalize her world
    d. to marry Uncle Andrew and settle down
    c. take over earth and make herself queen
    d. kidnap Uncle Andrew & bring him to Charn

17. One of the things that happens to Jadis on earth is:
    a. she becomes much nicer
    b. she is much smaller
    c. she is much meaner
    d. she has no power to turn people to dust

18. Digory becomes interested when he overhears his aunt saying that his mother could only be helped by:
    a. fruit from the land of youth
    b. a flower from Mt. Everest
    c. an undiscovered antibiotic
    d. a specialist from the United States

19. When Digory and Polly try to cut down on the damage the Witch is doing in their world by transporting her back to where she came from, they accidentally take with them:
    a. Uncle Andrew, Aunt Letty & the maid
    b. Uncle Andrew, store owner & the maid
    c. Uncle Andrew, the Cabby & the policeman
    d. Uncle Andrew, the Cabby & the horse

20. When they arrive in a new world, the difference in this place is:
    a. the sun is very bright
    b. it is completely dark
    c. there are two suns
    d. there are two moons

21. The suggestion made by the Cabby is:
    a. they should sing a hymn
    b. they should go to another world
    c. they should say a prayer
    d. they should put on a happy face

22. When Jadis tries to hit the Lion with the metal bar from the lamp-post, the result is:
    a. it knocks the lion unconscious
    b. it misses the lion altogether
    c. it bounces off the lion & grows a lamp-post
    d. it breaks apart and disintegrates

23. Uncle Andrew's plans for this world begin with:
    a. getting rid of the Witch
    b. killing the lion
    c. building a health resort
    d. setting up a tour guide service

24. Strawberry, the horse, has changed from:
    a. a tired workhorse into a unicorn
    b. a tired workhorse into a bird
    c. a tired workhorse to a young horse
    d. a tired workhorse into a kangaroo

25. When the animals see Uncle Andrew they:
    a. plant him in the ground
    b. try to feed him
    c. fence him in
    d. all of the above

26. When Digory goes to Aslan for help, Aslan:
    a. immediately agrees to help him
    b. sends him away
    c. tells him he has done too much evil
    d. forces him to be accountable for his actions

27. Aslan tells the animals that there will be a price to pay for the evil that has been brought into Narnia and:
    a. he will bear all of it
    b. the animals will take care of it
    c. Adam's race will play a part in it
    d. the Witch will pay the price

28. The statement made by Aslan about the price to be paid in the future is an example of:
    a. comic relief
    b. foreshadowing
    c. flashback
    d. figurative language

29. In order to make up for the wrong he has done in Narnia, Digory is required to:
    a. give up all he has
    b. find the Witch and destroy her
    c. spend the rest of his life in Narnia
    d. go to a garden and return with an apple

30. In order to help him get to his destination, Aslan provides Digory with:
    a. an army of dwarves
    b. a new car
    c. Strawberry, who has been given wings
    d. the ability to fly

31. When they stop for the night, the children discover Aslan has not provided them with:
    a. any food for their journey
    b. shelter from a storm
    c. a change of clothing
    d. none of the above

32. The children solve the previous problem when they find:
    a. some fruit in Digory's pocket & plant it
    b. some toffee in Polly's pocket & plant it
    c. an extra blanket in their saddlebags
    d. a tent

33. When they reach the garden they discover:
    a. Polly and Fledge can accompany Digory
    b. only Polly can accompany Digory
    c. only Digory can enter
    d. only the Witch can accompany Digory

34. When he finds the apple, Digory is faced with the temptation to:
    a. taste the apple
    b. give the apple to Polly
    c. plant the seeds
    d. throw the apple away

35. Jadis tries to convince Digory to:
    a. give the apple to her
    b. take the apple to his mother
    c. throw the apple away
    d. give the apple to Uncle Andrew

36. It was necessary for Digory to face this temptation because:
    a. he had never faced temptation before
    b. Aslan disliked him
    c. he failed to resist temptation with the bell
    d. Aslan had big plans for him

37. When Digory tells Aslan that Jadis has already eaten one of the apples, he tells Digory that:
    a. it won't work on Jadis
    b. she will live with eternal misery
    c. the fruit will not give Jadis eternal youth
    d. she will have knowledge of good & evil

The Magician's Nephew

38. Aslan explains to Digory that, if he had followed the advice Jadis gave him and taken the apple to his mother instead of Aslan, the consequences would be:
    a. his mother would live happily ever after
    b. his mother would immediately die
    c. Jadis would control him forever
    d. his mother would get well, but be miserable

39. The lesson to be learned from the apple is:
    a. obedience is always what is important
    b. never listen to the Witch
    c. eating apples is always important
    d. never give in to temptation

40. The seeds of the apple Digory takes back to earth grow into a tree and eventually:
    a. the wood is used to build a house
    b. the wood is used to make a bench
    c. the wood is used to make a wardrobe
    d. the wood is used for a bed

II. Matching: Place the letter of the correct answer in the blank:

1. ____ the Cabby   A. name given Uncle Andrew by the animals
2. ____ guinea pig   B. received a punishment after their first return from the other worlds
3. ____ Mrs. Lefay   C. name for Strawberry after he was given wings
4. ____ Uncle Andrew   D. became the first King of Narnia
5. ____ Aunt Letty   E. required to accept responsibility for sinful actions
6. ____ Fledge   F. person who gave magical sand to Uncle Andrew
7. ____ Aslan   G. thought at one point that Jadis might fall in love with him
8. ____ Brandy   H. first one sent to the Wood Between the Worlds
9. ____ Digory   I. woman of courage and integrity
10. ____ Polly   J. had compassionate tears for Digory's mother

III. Matching: Place the letter of the correct answer in the blank:

1. ____ Charn   A. protected by an incantation giving directions for entry
2. ____ Wood Between the Words   B. place where Digory's father was working
3. ____ Narnia   C. land around lamp-post that grew in Narnia
4. ____ Lantern Waste   D. Digory's family home – future entry into Narnia
5. ____ Archenland   E. very quiet, green land seemed to be in spring
6. ____ garden   F. land ruled by children of King Frank & Queen Helen

7. ____London   G. dying land formerly ruled by grim people

8. ____India   H. main setting for the story; Polly's home

9. ____country house   I. brought into being through Aslan's song

IV. Short Answer:

1. Throughout the book, the children learn things about the rings that Uncle Andrew did not know. List the facts they discover as they use the rings.

2. Which adult in the story has the purest heart? How do you know? How is this person rewarded by Aslan?

3. When the children go on their quest with Fledge, and they discover their lack of provisions, what does Fledge reveal to them about the character of Aslan? How does this compare to the nature of God?

4. Other than the instructions concerning the rings, what warning does Aslan give to Digory and Polly before sending them back to their own world? Consider the beginning of *The Lion, The Witch and The Wardrobe*. Thirty – forty years have passed, and Digory is now a middle-aged "eccentric professor" with whom the Pevensie children come to escape the horrors of World War II. How do you think Digory feels about the current situation his world is facing?

5. When Lucy goes through the wardrobe and discovers Narnia, the older children at first think she is losing her mind, and go to Professor Kirke for advice. Why doesn't Digory just tell them about his experiences in Narnia, rather than just telling them to trust Lucy?

ANSWERS TO TEST QUESTIONS
THE MAGICIAN'S NEPHEW

I. **Multiple Choice:**
1. d
2. b
3. c
4. b
5. d
6. c
7. a
8. b
9. d
10. b
11. c
12. a
13. d
14. c
15. d
16. c
17. d
18. a
19. d
20. b
21. a
22. c
23. b
24. c
25. d
26. d
27. c
28. b
29. d
30. c
31. a
32. b
33. c
34. a
35. b
36. c
37. b
38. d
39. a
40. c

II. **Matching:**
1. D
2. H
3. F
4. G
5. I
6. C
7. J
8. A
9. E
10. B

III. **Matching:**
1. G
2. E
3. F
4. C
5. F
6. A
7. H
8. B
9. D

IV. **Short Answer:**

1. A green ring takes the bearer away from the Wood Between the Worlds, while the yellow ring draws the bearer to that place. One does not have to actually put the ring on in order to be placed under its power. It is only necessary to touch it. Anyone who touches a person who is touching one of the rings will be taken with them when they are drawn to another world.

2. The Cabby is the adult with the purest heart. When Aslan talks to him, he reminds him that he knew him in our world as well as in Narnia. He is the first to realize they should sing a hymn when they first enter Narnia in the dark. Aslan rewards him by making him the King of Narnia.

3. Fledge tells them that, although Aslan could have supplied them with food for their journey, they did not ask for any, and he has the feeling that Aslan likes to be asked. Likewise, Scripture states that even though God knows our needs before we ask, He likes for us to come to Him in prayer with our needs.

4. Aslan warns Digory and Polly that, during their lifetime, there will be tyrants in their world who will not care any more for justice and joy and mercy than Jadis. As he watches the beginning of World War II, with Hitler trying to dominate the world and other dictators ruling in Russia, Italy and Japan, he must realize that Aslan's prophesy for earth has come to fulfillment. He must have some concerns as to whether or not this world will be able to continue, since Charn died.

5. When he realizes that Lucy has been drawn into Narnia, he must be aware that Aslan is drawing her, and that the fulfillment of Aslan's prophesy is nearing. If he is aware of the entire prophesy, he knows it will require all four children, and he would not want to frighten them away by trying to "explain" to them a world that is unexplainable. If they knew they would be required to battle a witch with powers beyond anything they could imagine, the children would be less likely to freely go through the wardrobe. It must occur to Digory that, if the conditions in this world point to the end of the world, and the children are being summoned to rescue Narnia, it may mean that he will be able to return to Narnia himself. Knowing the children already consider him "peculiar," he probably feels it wise to let the others follow Lucy into Narnia on their own. He has probably observed the children sufficiently to know that Lucy has the purest heart, the greatest zeal for Aslan, and will eventually persuade the others to follow her.

Magician's Nephew Vocab Chapt 1

Across
3. insane
5. characterized by wiliness and trickiness
6. run off or away; flee
7. disheveled; mussed
11. those who import or export secretly, illegally, or without paying duties required by law
12. expressing strong displeasure at something considered unjust, offensive, insulting

Down
1. futile
2. inventer
4. an incompetent or clumsy person
5. an often underground tank for storing water
8. admitting currents of air, usually uncomfortable
9. abominable; disagreeable
10. questionable

Magician's Nephew Vocab Chapt 1

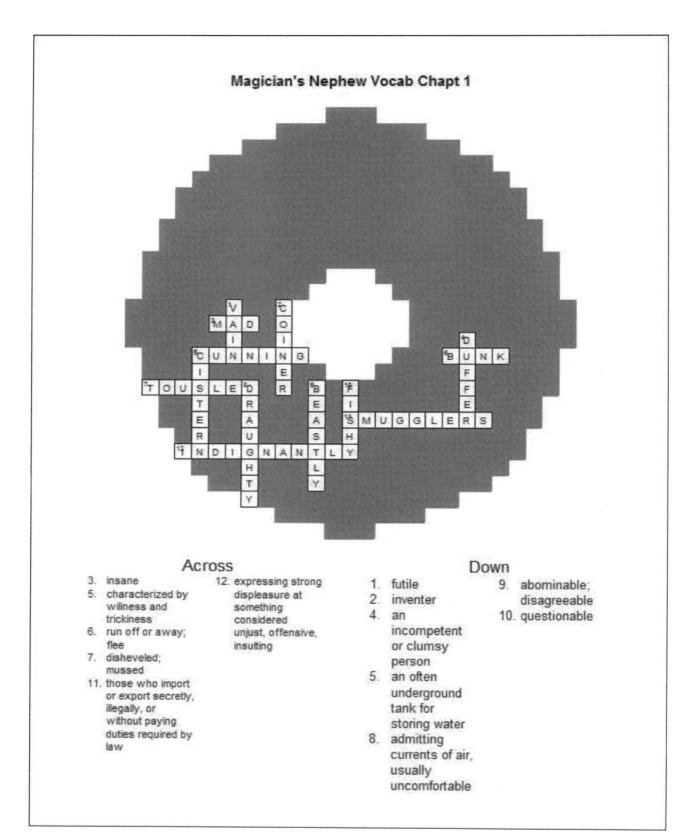

Across
3. insane
5. characterized by wiliness and trickiness
6. run off or away; flee
7. disheveled; mussed
11. those who import or export secretly, illegally, or without paying duties required by law
12. expressing strong displeasure at something considered unjust, offensive, insulting

Down
1. futile
2. inventor
4. an incompetent or clumsy person
5. an often underground tank for storing water
8. admitting currents of air, usually uncomfortable
9. abominable; disagreeable
10. questionable

Magician's Nephew Vocab Ch 2-3

Across

2. marked by intellectual depth or insight
5. a cleaning woman especially in a large building
7. a predetermined course of events
8. an institution for the care of the needy or sick and especially the insane
9. not clear, definite, or distinct
10. slang: to talk excessively
12. expert
13. peculiar; strange

Down

1. contrary to nature or reason; absurd
3. of a superior nature
4. the spirit or character of the ideal knight
6. those who are distinguished for wisdom
11. dignified; solemn

Magician's Nephew Vocab Ch 2-3

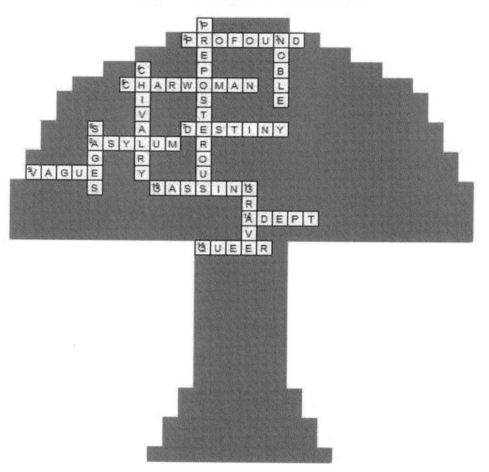

Across
2. marked by intellectual depth or insight
5. a cleaning woman especially in a large building
7. a predetermined course of events
8. an institution for the care of the needy or sick and especially the insane
9. not clear, definite, or distinct
10. slang: to talk excessively
12. expert
13. peculiar; strange

Down
1. contrary to nature or reason; absurd
3. of a superior nature
4. the spirit or character of the ideal knight
6. those who are distinguished for wisdom
11. dignified; solemn

Magician's Nephew Vocab Ch 4-6

Across

6. hopeless
8. pretending
9. having strong upright supports
11. violation of allegiance or trust
14. devilishly; excessively; extremely
15. morose; moody
16. total or partial obscuring of one heavenly body by another
17. a two-wheeled covered carriage with the driver's seat elevated at the rear

Down

1. magical spells
2. get possession of, obtain
3. a mass of snow, ice, earth, or rock sliding down a mountainside
4. stubborn
5. a servile dependent, follower or underling
7. familiar
9. peace
10. an outer garment worn especially by men
12. broken fragments especially of a destroyed buildings
13. foolish talk or action ; nonsense

Magician's Nephew Vocab Ch 4-6

Across
6. hopeless
8. pretending
9. having strong upright supports
11. violation of allegiance or trust
14. devilishly; excessively; extremely
15. morose; moody
16. total or partial obscuring of one heavenly body by another
17. a two-wheeled covered carriage with the driver's seat elevated at the rear

Down
1. magical spells
2. get possession of; obtain
3. a mass of snow, ice, earth, or rock sliding down a mountainside
4. stubborn
5. a servile dependent, follower or underling
7. familiar
9. peace
10. an outer garment worn especially by men
12. broken fragments especially of a destroyed buildings
13. foolish talk or action; nonsense

Magician's Nephew Vocab Ch 7-9

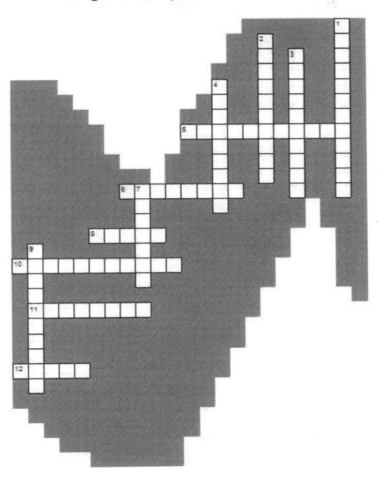

Across
5. rude; insolent
6. beating as if with a rod or whip
8. a strap or an iron catch between the shaft and harness on a drawn wagon, allowing the horse to stop or back up
10. a solution of ammonium carbonate in alcohol or ammonia water, used in smelling salts
11. choke; strangle
12. a lewd or brazen woman

Down
1. pretentious or excessive display
2. polite acts or expressions
3. odious; detestable; loathsome
4. rushing about wildly
7. an insane person
9. an institution for the treatment of chronic diseases or for medically supervised recuperation

Magician's Nephew Vocab Ch 7-9

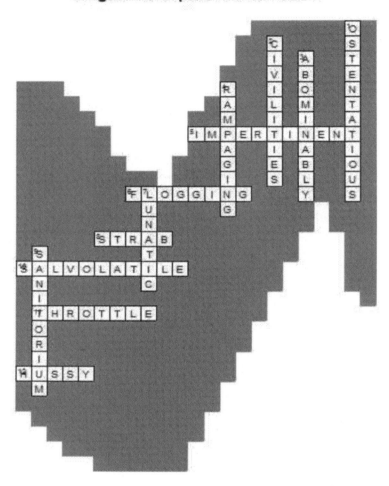

Across
5. rude; insolent
6. beating as if with a rod or whip
8. a strap or an iron catch between the shaft and harness on a drawn wagon, allowing the horse to stop or back up
10. a solution of ammonium carbonate in alcohol or ammonia water, used in smelling salts
11. choke; strangle
12. a lewd or brazen woman

Down
1. pretentious or excessive display
2. polite acts or expressions
3. odious; detestable; loathsome
4. rushing about wildly
7. an insane person
9. an institution for the treatment of chronic diseases or for medically supervised recuperation

Magician's Nephew Vocab Ch 10-11

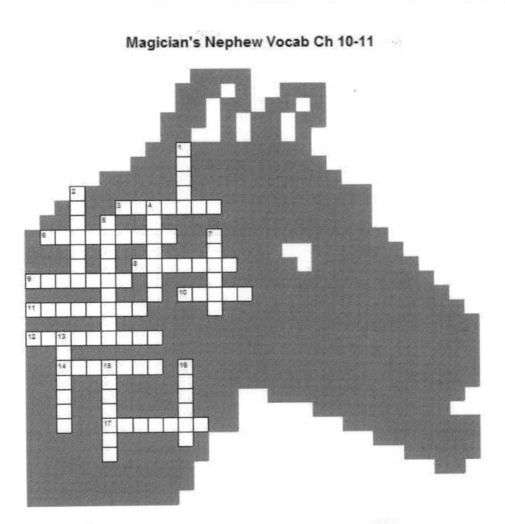

Across

3. a black and gray Old World crowlike bird
6. bewitched
8. to struggle against or over
9. fairness
10. lively; cheerful
11. first in time, place, or order
12. a cutting or contemptuous remark
14. pull something from
17. a native of London and especially of the East End of London

Down

1. one of the nymphs who lived in and presided over brooks, springs, and fountains
2. a dense growth of bushes or small trees
4. hold dear, treat with care and affection
5. of keen mind; shrewd
7. woodland creature depicted as having the pointed ears, legs, and short horns of a goat and fondness of unrestrained revelry
13. curb; restrain
15. an official body of lawmakers
16. a stiff felt hat with rounded crown and narrow brim

Magician's Nephew Vocab Ch 10-11

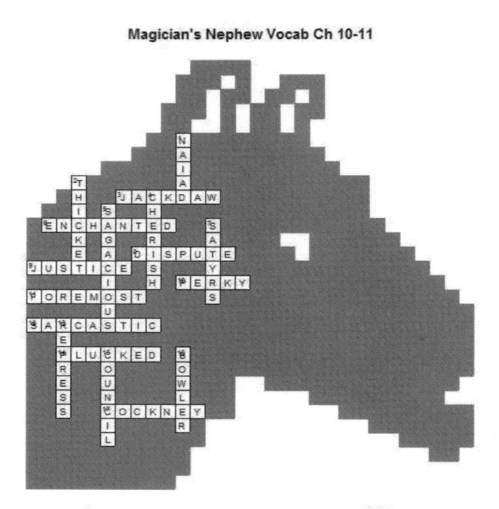

Across
3. a black and gray Old World crowlike bird
6. bewitched
8. to struggle against or over
9. fairness
10. lively; cheerful
11. first in time, place, or order
12. a cutting or contemptuous remark
14. pull something from
17. a native of London and especially of the East End of London

Down
1. one of the nymphs who lived in and presided over brooks, springs, and fountains
2. a dense growth of bushes or small trees
4. hold dear, treat with care and affection
5. of keen mind; shrewd
7. woodland creature depicted as having the pointed ears, legs, and short horns of a goat and fondness of unrestrained revelry
13. curb; restrain
15. an official body of lawmakers
16. a stiff felt hat with rounded crown and narrow brim

Magician's Nephew Vocab Ch 12-13

Across
4. hurry
5. a deep orange powder from the flower of a crocus used to color and flavor foods
6. leap vigorously especially by aid of the hands or a pole
7. a horse's 3-beat gait resembling but smother and slower than a gallop
9. fool
11. the upper layer of soil bound by grass and roots into a close mat
13. a prancing leap of a horse

Down
1. utter loss of hope
2. causing ruin
3. highly serious
7. steep rapids in a river
8. any of the lesser goddesses in ancient mythology represented as maidens living in the mountains, forests, meadows, and waters
10. start suddenly aside though fright
12. cry

Magician's Nephew Vocab Ch 12-13

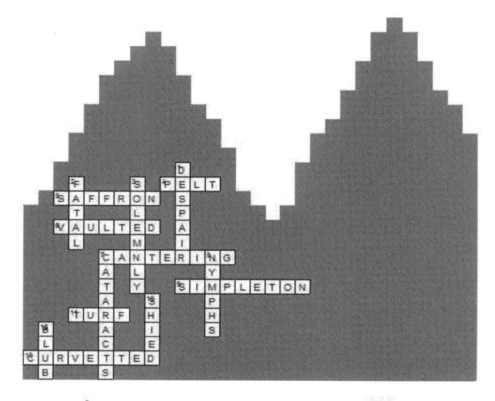

Across
4. hurry
5. a deep orange powder from the flower of a crocus used to color and flavor foods
6. leap vigorously especially by aid of the hands or a pole
7. a horse's 3-beat gait resembling but smother and slower than a gallop
9. fool
11. the upper layer of soil bound by grass and roots into a close mat
13. a prancing leap of a horse

Down
1. utter loss of hope
2. causing ruin
3. highly serious
7. steep rapids in a river
8. any of the lesser goddesses in ancient mythology represented as maidens living in the mountains, forests, meadows, and waters
10. start suddenly aside though fright
12. cry

Magician's Nephew Vocab Ch 14-15

Across
3. bedspread
4. excessively high opinion of one's self or ability
5. sickly; feeble; weak
7. two weeks
9. threw, hit, or propelled something in a high arc
10. wiliness and trickery
12. a burst of many things at once
13. a small flat or scooplike implement used in gardening

Down
1. the act or ceremony of crowning a monarch
2. attacked with bombs, shells, or missiles
4. a small enclosure or building usually for poultry
6. dislike greatly
8. rulers who govern oppressively or brutally
11. foolishness

Magician's Nephew Vocab Ch 14-15

Across
3. bedspread
4. excessively high opinion of one's self or ability
5. sickly; feeble; weak
7. two weeks
9. threw, hit, or propelled something in a high arc
10. wiliness and trickery
12. a burst of many things at once
13. a small flat or scooplike implement used in gardening

Down
1. the act or ceremony of crowning a monarch
2. attacked with bombs, shells, or missiles
4. a small enclosure or building usually for poultry
6. dislike greatly
8. rulers who govern oppressively or brutally
11. foolishness

SELECTED BIBLIOGRAPHY

Biographical Material

http://www.cslewis.org/resources/chronoccl.html. (2006).

Lindsley, Art. http://www.cslewisinstitute.org/pages/resources/cslewis/index.php. (2006).

Sayer, George. Jack: C. S. Lewis and His Times. San Francisco: Harper and Row, Publishers. 1988.

Dictionaries

Slater, Rosalie J. *Noah Webster's 1828 American Dictionary of the English Language.* (San Francisco:Foundation for American Christian Education); 1967 & 1995

Webster's Third International Dictionary (Springfield, MA: G & C. Merriam Co.); 1963.

Webster's Universal College Dictionary (New York:Gramercy Books); 1997.

http://www.thefreedictionary.com/html. (May 2006).

Printed in Great Britain
by Amazon